Fort I

MW00906736

Delǎplaine 2⊕18

LONG   WEEKEND   GUIDE

Andrew Delaplaine

A list of the author's other travel guides, as well as his political thrillers
and titles for children, can be found at the end of this book.

Senior Editors – **Renee & Sophie Delaplaine**
Senior Writer – **James Cubby**
Art Director – **Charles McGoldrick**

Gramercy Park Press
New York – London – Paris

Please submit corrections, additions or comments to
andrewdelaplaine@mac.com

TABLE OF CONTENTS

Chapter 1 – FIRST THINGS FIRST – 4
Why Fort Lauderdale?
Transportation & Tips for Getting Around
Specific Information During Your Visit
Visitors' Centers

Chapter 2 - LODGING – 8
Beach Area
Downtown
Airport Area
Gay Lodgings
Cruise Ship Departure Stays

Chapter 3 – RESTAURANTS – 22
Expensive
Moderate
Inexpensive
Sports Bars

Chapter 4 – NIGHTLIFE – 68

Chapter 5 – ATTRACTIONS – 75

Chapter 6 - SHOPPING & SERVICES – 86

INDEX – 95

OTHER BOOKS BY THE AUTHOR – 100

Chapter 1
WHY FORT
LAUDERDALE?

Fort Lauderdale, for good or ill, has always been defined not for what it is, really, as for what it lies between. About 40 miles to the north is Palm Beach. About 25 miles south is Miami. A million images flood the mind when you think of Miami. (Cocaine Cowboys, the Mariel Boatlift, South Beach, the nightlife, Little Havana, an international port and banking center.) Similarly, a million images leap into your mind when you conjure up Palm Beach (Worth Avenue, Cartier, the Kennedys, wealthy socialites, vast fortunes, elderly women with young gigolos.)

And Fort Lauderdale? What images jump into your mind when you first think of the town? Connie Francis and

"Where the Boys Are"? Spring Break? Sailboats?

Well, Fort Lauderdale has come a long way since that 1960 movie.

And the good thing that has made Fort Lauderdale so attractive for so long is that it is *not* Miami and it is *not* Palm Beach. It's just that "little bit of in between" that makes Fort Lauderdale so great. And, being in the middle of the Gold Coast, Fort Lauderdale is a perfect location if you like Miami or Palm Beach, but don't want to live there. You're just a few minutes away by I-95 or the Turnpike from posh Palm Beach or the nonstop excitement of Miami.

Wonderful smaller towns (Davie, Dania, Lauderdale-by-the-Sea, Lighthouse Point) offer extremely cheap housing (if you want to live here) and lodgings, if you're visiting. And you're close-close-close to all the action. (I know a lot of actors who live in these towns for the very reason that they are easily able to go to auditions in Miami or Palm Beach. When they get jobs, they're never too far away.)

Transportation & Tips for Getting Around

There are very few cities where I have to write such a short chapter about transit.

Here in Fort Lauderdale, there are no travel tips for "getting around." None.

In Broward County, you'll need a car, pure and simple, unless you plan to stick close to a spa or the beach (in which case, you merely use taxis—the major cab company here is **Yellow Cab – 954-777-7777**). The bus system is a joke, the Tri Rail system connecting you to Palm Beach and Miami also is a joke (you need a car to get to it), so you may just as well knuckle under and get a car.

The auto traffic in Fort Lauderdale is *horrendous*. Even worse than Miami some days (and that's saying something). Whenever I go to Fort Lauderdale, I try to leave Miami no later than 10 a.m. and get back before 3 p.m., thus avoiding the morning and afternoon traffic nightmares. So I'm always running up to Fort Lauderdale for lunch or dinner, but I do everything I can to avoid the peak driving times. You should too. Day in and day out, it's a constant nightmare, and I consider myself fortunate not to have to endure it the way so many commuters do.

So, get a car. If the weather's nice, get a convertible and enjoy it.

Always take a bottle or two of water with you when you drive around. In the summer, if you have a flat, you'll appreciate that water while you're waiting for roadside assistance.

And if you do experience car trouble, be wary of unscrupulous tow truck driver who appear out of the blue to lend you assistance. If they are not the people you called (like AAA), don't let them bullshit you into hooking up your car. There's a lot of scamming that goes on—once they get your car hooked up, they'll charge you a fortune before they unhook it. Some of these guys say they've been sent by the Highway Patrol to get your car out of the way, but it's all lies. Don't let them bully you.

RED LIGHT CAMERAS. Fort Lauderdale has installed a system of red light cameras. If you run a red light, the system takes a photo of your plate and you will be sent a ticket. (I think the current rate is $158.) It's a shameless ripoff, but that's the way it is. You'll see the cameras above the stop lights in the center of major intersections.

Specific Information During Your Visit

BROWARD-PALM BEACH *NEW TIMES*
www.broggwardpalmbeach.com
This weekly freebie paper is available on almost every
street corner in boxes—you definitely need to get a copy
to see what's going on the week or two you're in town.
Online you'll find thousands of listings that will help you
work your way through the town.

SUN-SENTINEL
www.sun-sentinel.com
This is the local daily newspaper, but only its Friday and
Sunday editions have information of use to the visitor. The
web site is a big help.

Visitors' Centers

THE GREATER FORT LAUDERDALE
CONVENTION & VISITORS BUREAU
954-765-4466.
www.sunny.org
Has complete listings.

Chapter 2
LODGING

BEACH AREA

It's very true what they say. Fort Lauderdale has a beach for everyone! After all, this is what you are really coming to Fort Lauderdale to enjoy. Isn't it?

ATLANTIC HOTEL

601 N. Ft. Lauderdale Beach Blvd, Fort Lauderdale: 954-567-8020

www.atlantichotelfl.com

This smallish property (124 rooms & suites) right on the water has a lot to recommend it: a causal décor that remains stylish while not being stuffy like the **W** or the

Ritz. (About half the rooms have full kitchens). Also has the **Spa Atlantic**, sea-and-citrus inspired day spa. As a splendidly relaxing destination, his sanctuary uses products made from natural ingredients. Deep-tissue massage, revitalizing body scrub in one of 8 private treatment rooms, Swedish massage, in-suite massages, aromatherapy massage. Also, a couples treatment room. Also offers a spectrum of refreshing facial, professional salon services and beauty treatments.

BAHIA MAR BEACH RESORT

801 Seabreeze Blvd., Fort Lauderdale: 954-764-2233
www.bahiamarhotel.com
This 40-acre beachfront retreat is within walking distance of Las Olas Boulevard with the area's shopping, dining and **Riverwalk** entertainment.

COURTYARD BY MARRIOTT

440 Seabreeze Blvd., Fort Lauderdale Beach: 954-524-8733
www.marriott.com
If you want the same-old, same-old, here it is.

GALT VILLAS

3621 N. Ocean Blvd., Fort Lauderdale: 954-565-1795
www.galtvillas.com
Right across the street from the beach. Great rates; rooms and efficiencies; daily, weekly, monthly; pool, 27" TVs with 70 channels; in-room coffee maker with free coffee; mini-fridge & microwave; rollaway beds, cribs, ironing boards, coin laundry, free Internet station.

GRANADA INN

3011 Granada St., Fort Lauderdale: 954-463-2032
www.thegranadainn.com
The Granada Inn is an open-balcony Caribbean art deco style **bed and breakfast** located just a few short steps from

the beach. The continental breakfast is served poolside, which is surrounded by palm trees and a tropical garden.

HYATT REGENCY PIER 66
2301 S.E. 17th St. Cswy., Fort Lauderdale: 954-525-6666
http://www.HyattRegencyPierSixty-Six.com
The famous **Pier 66** property with its distinctive rooftop restaurant. Newly renovated (2009) and located in a 22-acre, lushly landscaped property 3 miles from the airport, 3 blocks from the beach (they have a free shuttle) and 10 minutes from downtown. Has a very impressive Spa. (There's a Sunday Brunch in the restaurant on top that's as real treat. The views are outstanding.) One of the big treats about this place is you've got lot of marina action. Fort Lauderdale is famous as a yachting center (unlike Miami), so you're constantly surrounded by boat people. A lot of them hang out here.

LAGO MAR RESORT
http://www.lagomar.com/
1700 S. Ocean Ln., Fort Lauderdale: 954-523-6511
This luxury resort features 475 feet of private sandy beach,
a 9,000 sq. ft. swimming lagoon and 2 tennis courts. Play
a game of chess on the life-sized outdoor chess set. It's
situated between Lake Mayan and the ocean on a 10-acre
plot that's lushly landscaped. Great yacht watching. Lots
of the rooms and suites here have full kitchens. Has lots of
on-site activities (putt-putt golf, tennis, beach volleyball,
shuffleboard, playground and that very huge pool), making
it a popular destination for families. Also excellent on-site
dining.

MARRIOTT'S BEACHPLACE TOWERS
21 S. Fort Lauderdale Beach Blvd., Fort Lauderdale: 954-
525-4440
www.marriott.com
Between the waters of the Atlantic & Intracoastal
Waterway, Marriott's BeachPlace Towers gives you the
full-on Marriott treatment. They have spacious one- and
two-bedroom villas or deluxe guestrooms situated atop
three floors of retail shops & restaurants. (The villas
feature separate living and dining areas, large master suites
with king beds and oversized soaking tubs, full kitchens
with cookware and tableware, utility rooms with washer/
dryer.)

THE PILLARS

111 N. Birch Rd., Fort Lauderdale: 954-467-9639
www.pillarshotel.com

Hidden away off the beach is this genuine find. Walk out
to the tropically landscaped pool area that overlooks the
Intracoastal. No better place to relax than this place, and
once you've stayed here, you'll be telling everybody you
know about it in a way that will cause everyone to envy
you. It's places like this that make you want to avoid the
Ritz-Carlton and the **W** and all the other properties in the
thick of things. Why? Because this place is different. You
get the feeling (OK, it's fleeting) that you've gone back in
time to some Colonial outpost in the Caribbean. This
impression is enhanced when you get a room with French
doors. (Ask for one.) The furnishings are refined (rich dark

woods, elegant upholstery) and comfortable. There's a restaurant here where it's divine to sit at night overlooking the Intracoastal as the yachts go by. (None of your noisy beach traffic here, thank you very much.) Eatery is called the **Secret Garden**. Breakfast and lunch are served only to hotel guests. At dinner they allow outsiders to come in, those who are members of the Secret Garden Society, the hotel's private dining club. (Call or email them at secretgarden@pillarshotel.com to see if they'll let you squeeze in for dinner.)

RITZ-CARLTON FORT LAUDERDALE RESORT
1 N. Fort Lauderdale Beach Blvd., Fort Lauderdale Beach: 954-465-2300
www.ritzcarlton.com
Ritz-Carlton Spa (with 8500 square feet) features private treatment rooms, separate lounges for men and women, cardiovascular and strength equipment in the fitness room; 11 treatment rooms including private couple's treatment suite; private massage areas and Jacuzzis on the tropical

pool deck; fitness center with Technogym cardiovascular and strength equipment; Spa boutique. 24 hour business center. Many of the niceties you'd expect from a Ritz-Carlton property. A private little skywalk that takes you to the beach. A huge wine cellar. A "pampered pooch" special for dogs (under 25 lbs.) offers a special dog bed in your room so Fido won't feel left out of all the fun. The excellent **Via Luna** restaurant is located here.

SEA LORD HOTEL & SUITES
4140 El Mar Dr., Lauderdale-by-the-Sea: 954-776-1505
www.sealordhotel.com
On 150 feet of beach. The pool deck overlooks the ocean. This property was renovated in 2002. Perfectly nice mid-range property.

SEVILLE HOTEL
3020 Seville St., Fort Lauderdale: 954-463-7212
http://www.sevilleatthebeach.com/
Located in the heart of the beach district and just steps away from restaurants, entertainment, water taxis and shopping. The Seville offers efficiencies & apartments with fully equipped kitchens as well as hotel rooms with fridge & microwaves.

TROPIROCK RESORT
2900 Belmar St., Fort Lauderdale: 954-565-5790
www.tropirock.com
A 3 or 4 minute walk from the beach. The Tropirock features handcrafted designer furnishings, colorful Caribbean art fusion and a highly trained multilingual staff. The landscaping is unique in the sense that it's totally UN-corporate. Funky. Exotic. Winding pathways take to you citrus trees, banana trees and coconut palms, papaya, fragrant jasmine and blooming passion vines. Throughout the property you'll run into a series of mosaics that add to the artistic sensibility they're going for here. Terra cotta

suns, chips of reflective glass, broken dishware, seashells and chunks of coral in a stucco mix all surrounded by lush tropical landscaping.

W HOTEL FORT LAUDERDALE
401 N. Fort Lauderdale Beach Blvd., Fort Lauderdale: 954-414-8200
www.starwoodhotels.com
Hard to call it a "boutique" hotel with over 400 rooms, but it tries to be one while trading on its endlessly hip image. The concierge with the "whenever/whatever" service. Reminds me of that Noel Coward song, "The Passenger's Always Right," with the lyric: "The passenger's always right, my dear / the passenger's always right. / The son of a bitch is probably rich, / so smile with all your might." But all cattiness aside, the place is a dream. Right on the water. Beautifully designed rooms. Has **Steak 954** on site, as well as luxurious **Bliss Spa**.

WESTIN BEACH RESORT FORT LAUDERDALE

321 N. Fort Lauderdale Beach Blvd., Fort Lauderdale:
954-467-1111
www.westin.com

Tropically decorated rooms, 2 pools, recreation program, pool bar & grill, 2 lounges and live entertainment nightly. From the third-floor pool deck overlooking the water, there's a skywalk that you use to get to the beach. There's a **Heavenly Spa by Westin**, a 6,500-square-foot space with separate men's and women's Jacuzzis, steam rooms, and locker rooms. Spa treatments before or after exercise—the Heavenly Spa is located on the resort's first floor right across from the WestinWORKOUT Gym. Great place for the athletic among you. A short drive away is the **Jimmy Evert Tennis Center**, an outstanding public tennis center with 18 lighted clay courts and 3 hard courts, plus locker rooms, a lounge, pro shop, racquet re-stringing, and more. Refine your game with expert private lessons, or just practice your swings on your own by renting a ball machine. There's also the **Westin Kids Club**. On arrival, kids from four to 12 years old get an adventure-bound amenity bag to get them excited about their visit. The hotel has a "Discovery Room" where endless diversions from board games, arts and crafts, and even a Nintendo Wii will keep them occupied for hours. Healthy meals and snacks are provided, and a professional staff supervises a range of activities, including off-site excursions—so parents can relax and enjoy the resort themselves, worry-free. **WestinWORKOUT Gym** offers 1,425 square feet of space: a full array of strength-training equipment and free weights; cardio machines—treadmills, elliptical trainers, step machines, and stationary bikes all offer personal flat screen TVs. Ocean views out the windows offer further inspiration. The gym is open 24 hours a day to resort guests 16 years and older, complimentary and accessible with any guest room key. Towels and headphones are also provided.

DOWNTOWN AREA

The downtown area, especially around Las Olas Boulevard, has seen quite a bit of development in the past decade, and now hosts many new hotels and high-rise condominium developments. The downtown area is the largest in Broward County. My favorite hotel is still the quaint and charming **Riverside**. It's been upgraded, renovated and I'm not too pleased with the public rooms, but what the hell. I always get a room in the old section of the property.

HAMPTON INN FT. LAUDERDALE DOWNTOWN
250 N. Andrews Ave., Fort Lauderdale: 954-924-2700
www.hamptoninn3.hilton.com
The Hampton Inn Ft. Lauderdale Downtown features room service, a pool area, a multi-lingual staff and an exercise room. But boring, boring, boring.

RIVERSIDE HOTEL
620 E. Las Olas Blvd., Fort Lauderdale: 954-467-0671
www.riversidehotel.com
If you're going to be downtown, by all means stay here. It used to be my favorite hotel in Fort Lauderdale (that's not on the beach). Built in 1936, it's the oldest hotel in town, and they've added a 12-floor tower, but I prefer the older rooms. They call them "traditional rooms." Still, the rooms in the tower (big at 500 square feet) offer commanding views of the New River and all of downtown. I'm not at all happy with the way they've "upgraded" the dining room and the bars. Everything's ugly and generic, but it's still better than most places. And you're in the middle of Las Olas, the only really interesting street with any character in the whole town.

AIRPORT AREA

The Fort Lauderdale Hollywood International Airport serves millions of travellers from all over the world. Also known as FLL, the airport is ideally located in the heart of Broward County just minutes from Fort Lauderdale and white sandy beaches.

HOLIDAY INN FORT LAUDERDALE AIRPORT
2905 Sheridan St., Hollywood: 954-925-9100
www.holidayinn.com
This hotel features a tropical waterfall pool and a shuttle is available to the port.

GAY LODGINGS

Greater Fort Lauderdale has more than 150 gay-owned establishments including hotels, bars, clubs and restaurants, as well as three gay and lesbian publications and the largest Metropolitan Community Church congregation in the United States. While Fort Lauderdale is full of gay people, the focal point is Wilton Manors and Oakland Park. (These lodgings are either gay owned, gay operated or gay-friendly.)

THE ALCAZAR RESORT
555 N. Birch Rd., Fort Lauderdale: 954-563-6819
http://www.alcazarresort.com
The Alcazar is a gay males only resort featuring a clothing optional courtyard 24-hour heated pool. Formerly **Sea Chateau Motel**.

CAMBRIA SUITES
141 SW 19th Court, Dania Beach: 954-889-2600
www.cambriasuitesfortlauderdale.com
All suite hotel in Dania Beach. Oversized suites with luxurious bedding and upscale amenities like flat-screen televisions and spa-like baths featuring Bath and Body Works amenities.

CORAL REEF GUESTHOUSE
2609 N.E. 13th Ct., Fort Lauderdale: 954-568-0292
http://www.coralreefguesthouse.com
Gay-owned and operated, offering male accommodations close to the beach, restaurants and the Galleria Mall. Rooms are tastefully decorated, and overlook the clothing optional heated pool and 14-man Jacuzzi.

CRUISE SHIP DEPARTURE STAYS
Port Everglades is the huge cruise port at Fort Lauderdale, Florida. The popular departure port serves millions of smiling cruise passengers every year.

RED CARPET INN
2460 W. State Rd. 84, Fort Lauderdale: 954-792-4700
www.redcarpetinns.com
The Red Carpet Inn features a pool area and airport transportation.

HOLIDAY INN EXPRESS AIR AND SEA PORT
1150 W. State Rd. 84, Fort Lauderdale: 954-828-9905
www.hiexpress.com
Just a mile from the Fort Lauderdale - Hollywood Int'l Airport (FLL).
Every morning the property offers free USA Today and the complimentary, hot Express Start Breakfast Bar with delicious cinnamon rolls.

FORT LAUDERDALE AIRPORT/CRUISE PORT INN
1800 S. Federal Hwy., Fort Lauderdale: 954-767-8700
http://www.comfortsuites.com/
This hotel offers free airport and cruise port transportation,
a free expanded deluxe continental breakfast featuring a
Belgium Waffle station and is within walking distance to
restaurants and shopping.

**CROWNE PLAZA FORT LAUDERDALE AIRPORT /
CRUISE PORT**
455 State Rd. 84, Fort Lauderdale: 954-523-8080
www.crowneplaza.com
This hotel features room service, a swimming pool, airport
transportation and a multi-lingual staff.

Chapter 3
RESTAURANTS

There's no question that Fort Lauderdale has an abundance of dining opportunities situated on the water. You'd think in Florida that this would normally be the case, but it is not. In South Beach, let's say, there's only a handful of restaurants on the water. (All those restaurants lining Ocean Drive? They're all a five-minute walk across the park and beach to the water.)

But here in Fort Lauderdale, it's all about the water. You have restaurants actually on the beach. You have them in marinas overflowing with yachts from around the world. You have them on the Waterway.

EXPENSIVE

15TH STREET FISHERIES
1900 SE 15th St., Fort Lauderdale: 954-763-2777
http://www.15streetfisheries.com
CUISINE: Seafood
DRINKS: Full Bar
SERVING: Lunch/ Dinner
Right on the water with amazing views, this place is cozy

yet unpretentious. The lounge has a lower priced menu (than the room upstairs) that includes alligator burgers. The staff is friendly and knowledgeable, and if the menu seems a little pricey, remember that salad and an appetizer are included. $$$$

3030 OCEAN
3030 Holiday Dr., Fort Lauderdale: 954-765-3030
http://www.3030ocean.com
CUISINE: Seafood
DRINKS: Full Bar
SERVING: Dinner
Located in the Harbour Beach Marriott, at the helm of this restaurant is runner-up to *Hell's Kitchen,* Paula da Silva. Here she proves to be a winner with her progressive yet tasty menu. The tuna tartare? Best in town. The menu changes often as she likes to keep serving the freshest seafood with the freshest ingredients possible. $$$$

ANTHONY'S RUNWAY 84
330 State Road 84, Fort Lauderdale: 954-467-8484
http://runway-84.com
CUISINE: Italian
DRINKS: Full Bar
SERVING: Lunch/Dinner
This place has a feel of old Fort Lauderdale; that's a good thing. You must have the warm bread served with a cheese and olive oil dip that's to die for. Also on the menu are pizzas, but your best bet is to stick with the traditional Italian favorites. $$$$

ACQUARIO
LAGO MAR RESORT
http://www.lagomar.com/
1700 S. Ocean Ln., Fort Lauderdale: 954-523-6511
CUISINE: Varied; they call it "American bistro."
DRINKS: Full bar.
SERVING: dinner nightly.
Really excellent eatery here at Lago Mar, whatever the hell they call the cuisine. Try the butternut squash ravioli, pan roasted chicken, garlic lemon basil sauce ($22), the cherrywood plank salmon, pomegranate honey glazed, coarse boursin cheese grits ($22), shrimp & mussel garganelli with wilted greens, lemongrass lobster sauce ($29), or the hog snapper, cashew crusted, plantain jasmine rice, citrus butter sauce ($29). Or, really decadent: braised boneless short ribs, with root mashed, lemongrass Myers rum sauce ($32). The desserts are great, but skip them.

BISTRO MEZZALUNA
1821 SE 10th Ave., Fort Lauderdale: 954-522-9191
http://www.bistromezzaluna.com
CUISINE: Italian/ Seafood
DRINKS: Full Bar
SERVING: Dinner
Definitely a great place located in Fort Lauderdale's

yachting district. Here you will dine among yacht crew and boat captains. The seafood is fresh, the service is good, the prices are steep. $$$$

CAFÉ MARTORANO

3343 E. Oakland Park Blvd., Fort Lauderdale: 954-561-2554
http://www.cafemartorano.com
CUISINE: Italian
DRINKS: Full Bar
SERVING: Dinner
OK, so the kitschy, storefront location doesn't impress anyone; but the food certainly will. Loud and lively, this place serves up such good Italian fare that people will wait up to 2 hours for a table. Oh, and pay attention to who's sitting at the table next to you; celebrities are known to stop by when in town. $$$$

CAFE VICO

1125 N Federal Hwy, Fort Lauderdale: 954-565-9681
http://www.cafevicorestaurant.com
CUISINE: Italian
DRINKS: Full Bar
SERVING: Lunch/ Dinner
Although this place is pricey, some would argue it's the best Italian food they've had, so it's worth it. The lasagna is particularly good. Come early because this place fills up quickly. Another must-have: the crème brulee. $$$$

CASA D'ANGELO

1201 N. Federal Hwy, Fort Lauderdale: 954-564-1234
http://www.casa-d-angelo.com
CUISINE: Italian
DRINKS: Full Bar
SERVING: Dinner
Tuscan style Italian food served up by friendly, knowledgeable staff. Take note: everything here is

homemade and you can certainly taste it. Gnocchi is a standout, as is the steak Florentine (that you don't see very often these days), the snapper oreganata for something light but full-flavored and the fettuccine with roasted veal ragu top my list. Extensive wine list. $$$$

CHIMA BRAZILIAN STEAKHOUSE
2400 E Las Olas Blvd., Fort Lauderdale: 954-712-0580
http://chima.cc
CUISINE: Brazilian Steakhouse
DRINKS: Full Bar
SERVING: Dinner
Mediocre at best. The salad bar is not very good compared to other local steakhouses of this type. Service is not very attentive and it can be quite loud. $$$$

JWB PRIME STEAK
1111 N. Ocean Dr, Hollywood, 954-874-4462
www.jwbrestaurant.com
CUISINE: Steakhouse/Seafood
DRINKS: Full bar
SERVING: Dinner
PRICE RANGE: $$$
Steakhouse also known for its high quality seafood
selection. When you spot the humongous flip-flop that
signals you've arrived at Jimmy Buffet's Margaritaville,
you'll know you're close to JWB, which is next door.
Browse the huge raw bar that greets you when you enter.
Check out the spear-caught fish-of-the-day that they claim.
(I've always been skeptical that these selections were
really spear-caught.) Favorites: Paella and Lobster sushi
roll.

LOBSTER BAR SEA GRILLE
450 E Las Olas Blvd, Ft Lauderdale, 954-772-2675
www.buckheadrestaurants.com/lobster-bar-sea-grille
CUISINE: Seafood / Steakhouse
DRINKS: Full Bar
SERVING: Dinner nightly, Lunch weekdays
PRICE RANGE: $$$$

Modern-contemporary eatery (glistening white marble bar-top; waiters in white shirts & black vests; an oyster-appetizer kitchen in the middle of the dining room) with a creative menu of seafood and steaks. Menu favorites include: Local Snapper and Wild New Zealand Fresh Catch. Of course, they are known for their lobster dishes. As for the side dishes, the cauliflower gratin was tasty with lots of cheese.

STEAK 954
W Hotel
401 N. Fort Lauderdale Beach Blvd., Fort Lauderdale: 954-414-8333
http://www.steak954.com
CUISINE: Steakhouse
DRINKS: Full Bar
SERVING: Breakfast/ Lunch/ Dinner
Located in the very trendy W Hotel on Ft. Lauderdale Beach, this place is every bit tasteful as it is playful.
This steakhouse also has seafood, sandwiches and a raw bar on their menu. The centerpiece of the restaurant? A mesmerizing reef aquarium filled with jellyfish. Like we said, playful. $$$$

SUSHI ROCK CAFE

1515 E Las Olas Blvd., Fort Lauderdale: 954-462-5541
CUISINE: Sushi
DRINKS: Beer/ Wine
SERVING: Dinner
Just your average sushi restaurant. The food is average, the ambience is average and parking can be a problem. You decide. $$$

VALENTINO'S CUCINA ITALIANA

620 S Federal Hwy, Fort Lauderdale: 954-523-5767
www.valentinocucinaitaliana.com
CUISINE: Italian
DRINKS: Beer / Wine
SERVING: Dinner
Amazing northern Italian cuisine. The staff is very friendly and knowledgeable. This a great "special occasion" restaurant. They have a great wine list but if you're not too familiar with Italian wines, the staff here will guide you to make the perfect selection. $$$$

WILD SEA OYSTER BAR & GRILLE

620 E Las Olas Blvd, Ft Lauderdale, 954-467-2555
www.wildsealasolas.com
CUISINE: Seafood / Steakhouse
DRINKS: Full Bar
SERVING: Dinner nightly
PRICE RANGE: $$$
Located at the **Riverside Hotel**, this upscale seafood eatery offers an impressive menu of items like swordfish, grouper, wreckfish. Raw bar and wine list featuring more than 200 labels. There's also a delicious beef tenderloin with mushroom madeira jus. Late-night lounge vibe.

MODERATE

ASIA BAY
1111 E Las Olas Blvd., Fort Lauderdale: 954-848-9900
http://www.asiabayrestaurants.com
CUISINE: Sushi/ Japanese/ Thai
DRINKS: Beer/ Wine
SERVING: Lunch/ Dinner
Cute restaurant with an option to sit by the water. The sushi is excellent and the chef gets very creative with the Thai dishes. $$$

B'STRO ON THE BEACH

999 Fort Lauderdale Blvd., Fort Lauderdale: 954-389-1919
www.bhotelsandresorts.com
CUISINE: International
DRINKS: Beer/ Wine
SERVING: Breakfast/ Lunch/ Dinner
With a little bit of everything on the menu, you are sure to
find something to please you. They have mostly American,
French and Italian dishes. The atmosphere is very "South
Beach" and the staff friendly, but they could use a bit more
training (which can also be said about South Beach, now
that I think about it). $$$

BILLY'S STONE CRAB

400 N. Ocean Dr, Hollywood, 954-923-2300
www.crabs.com
CUISINE: Seafood
DRINKS: Full bar
SERVING: Lunch/Dinner
PRICE RANGE: $$$
Popular eatery for several decades offering a wide variety
of fresh seafood including fresh stone crabs, lobster
tails, King Crab legs, mahi-mahi, grouper, snapper, and
Norwegian Salmon. Seating inside and out by the water on
the Intracoastal. Upstairs it's a good deal fancier and you
can expect a fine dining experience. Downstairs it's ultra
casual. They offer a different "all-you-can-eat" dinner 7
nights a week that's a bargain.

BLUE MOON FISH CO.
4405 W. Tradewinds Ave, Lauderdale by the Sea, 954-267-9888
www.bluemoonfishco.com
CUISINE: Seafood
DRINKS: Full bar
SERVING: Lunch/Dinner
PRICE RANGE: $$$
Bright and spacious eatery overlooking the Intracoastal Waterway serves up food from an impressive menu. They cover all the bases here, and that might explain why they've been in business so long. They have a great happy hour. They have a great raw bar selection. They have a great weekend brunch. They have a great water view. They have wine dinners. They have a friendly staff. Menu picks: Fish Ceviche & Conch and Lump Crab and Roasted Corn Black Grouper. Dessert lovers should order the Icky Sticky (white chocolate bread pudding with junky monkey ice cream).

BOATYARD
1555 SE 17th St, Fort Lauderdale, 954-525-7400
www.boatyard.restaurant
CUISINE: Seafood
DRINKS: Full bar
SERVING: Lunch & Dinner daily
PRICE RANGE: $$$
Expansive restaurant with indoor and outdoor service
overlooking the water. Relaxed Florida nautical-themed
eatery that's a great date night pick featuring an open
kitchen and raw bar cart. But lunch is just as good an
option because you get great daytime views of the
Intracoastal. Menu of fresh seafood. Menu favorites: St.
Bart's Ceviche and Fresh Grouper. Happy hour specials.
The food here is good, not great, just good. Stick to the
fish, it's fresh. Their daily soup, a seafood chowder, seems
like everything that was left over from the night before was
thrown into a pot and cooked. (And I'm not saying that's a
bad thing, but a good thing.) Those of you old enough will
remember the Bimini Boatyard. This is the same location
spruced up quite nicely. The food is superlative compared
to those bygone days of fried fish platters and other crap.
You'll love this place.

BURLOCK COAST SEAFARE & SPIRITS
1 N Fort Lauderdale Beach Blvd, Fort Lauderdale, 954-
302-6460
www.ritzcarlton.com/en/hotels/florida/fort-lauderdale/
dining/burlock-coast-seafare-spirits
CUISINE: American/Seafood
DRINKS: Full bar
SERVING: Breakfast, Lunch & Dinner
PRICE RANGE: $$
Popular seafood eatery set in first floor of Ritz Carlton
Fort Lauderdale. Menu favorites include: Snapper Ceviche
and Black Grouper. The bar specializes in rum featuring a
variety of crafted cocktails.

CAFE SEVILLE

2768 E Oakland Park Blvd., Fort Lauderdale: 954-565-1148

http://www.cafeseville.com

CUISINE: Spanish

DRINKS: Beer/ Wine

SERVING: Dinner

Small and charming, the people here really know what they are doing. Absolutely everything on the menu is delicious. Check out the daily specials, sometimes they have rabbit. The staff is very friendly and don't be surprised if the owner stops by your table to say hello. You will not be disappointed. $$$

CANYON RESTAURANT

1818 E Sunrise Blvd., Fort Lauderdale: 954-765-1950

http://www.canyonfl.com

CUISINE: American

DRINKS: Full Bar

SERVING: Dinner

Quiet and cozy, this place does not take reservations. On the weekends there will be a wait. Excellent food . Must haves: prickly pear margarita and the bread pudding. $$$

CAP'S PLACE

2765 NE 28th Ct, Lighthouse Point, 954-941-
www.capsplace.com
CUISINE: Seafood
DRINKS: Full Bar
SERVING: Dinner nightly except Monday, when they are
closed.
PRICE RANGE: $$$
They've been dishing up fresh caught fish in this odd
location since 1930. Everybody who's been in Florida for a
long time has probably been to Cap's Place. If you haven't,
definitely put it on your bucket list. To get here, you have
to drive through a residential section of Lighthouse Point
to get to a wharf where you hop aboard a 25-foot long boat
that transports you across Lake Placid to the ramshackle
restaurant that looks like they haven't touched it since
President Roosevelt ate here with Winston Churchill in the
1940s. This landmark eatery offers a great menu featuring
seafood favorites like dolphin, wahoo, cobia, snapper,
lobster and stone crab. (The crab cake starter is among
the best I've ever had and the bacon-wrapped scallops are
really good.) After visiting this place, you'll definitely tell
your friends about it. Free parking at the wharf.

CARLOS & PEPE'S 17TH ST CANTINA

1302 SE 17th St., Fort Lauderdale: 954-467-8335
http://www.carlosandpepesfl.com
CUISINE: Tex Mex
DRINKS: Full Bar
SERVING: Dinner
If you like Tex Mex, you will probably like this place. The
service is a little slow and the staff is not very friendly,
except for the bartenders. It's best to sit at the bar and eat.
$$$

D'ANGELO RISTORANTE
1 N Federal Hwy, Fort Lauderdale: 954-564-1234
http://www.casa-d-angelo.com
CUISINE: Italian
DRINKS: Full Bar
SERVING: Dinner
Very good Italian food in a comfortable setting. The bar area is a little small. The food is exceptional, it's very difficult to find good Italian food but this place makes it. The wine list is extensive. $$$

CASABLANCA CAFE
3049 Alhambra St., Fort Lauderdale: 954-764-3500
http://www.casablancacafeonline.com
CUISINE: Mediterranean
DRINKS: Full Bar
SERVING: Lunch/ Dinner
What makes this place great is their location. Situated in a Spanish style building right across from the ocean, here you will enjoy both the views and the passersby. The food is just OK and the service is hit or miss. $$$

CHRISTINA WAN'S MANDARIN HO

664 N Federal Hwy, Fort Lauderdale: 954
http://www.christinawans.com
CUISINE: Chinese
DRINKS: Beer/ Wine
SERVING: Lunch/ Dinner
Really, really good Chinese food and reasc
Christina is usually right there to great you as you come in.
Comfy booths and tables make this a must-visit if you're
up for Chinese. $$

DOWNTOWNER

10 S. New River Dr. E., Fort Lauderdale: 954-463-9800
www.downtownersaloon.com
CUISINE: American; sports bar pub food
DRINKS: Full Bar
SERVING: Brunch/ Lunch/ Dinner/ Late Night
It's a little hard to describe this place, the food is really
good and you can catch your favorite team on any of the
many flat screens. Each night is a different specialty:
Mondays is steak night, Tuesday is ribs night… you get the
picture. Particularly good is the all-you-can-eat crab legs
on Sunday nights. $$

EL TAMARINDO CAFÉ

233 W. State Road 84, Fort Lauderdale: 954-467-5114
www.eltamarindocafe.com
CUISINE: Salvadorean/ Latin
DRINKS: Full Bar
SERVING: Breakfast/ Lunch/ Dinner
Who would think that the best Salvadorean food would be
in Fort Lauderdale? This place serves traditional favorites
like *pupusas* (corn tortillas stuffed with pork, beans,
cheese or mixed), hearty beef soup, or *tamal de elote* (a
delicious sweet corn tamale). White tablecloths and cheery,
courteous service combine to make this a magnate for
Latin food lovers. $$

EDUARDO DE SAN ANGEL

2822 E. Commercial Blvd, Fort Lauderdale: 954-772-4731
http://www.eduardodesanangel.com
CUISINE: Mexican
DRINKS: Beer/ Wine
SERVING: Lunch/ Dinner
Gourmet Mexican food at its best. This is not Mexican
like you're used to, it's better. From their *jaibas rellenas*
(stuffed Florida blue crab) to the ancho chile flavored

crepe. Oh and yes, here you will also find *mole poblano*, a Mexican favorite. $$$

GILBERT'S 17TH STREET GRILL
1821 Cordova Rd., Fort Lauderdale: 954-768-8990
http://www.gilberts17thstgrill.com
CUISINE: American
DRINKS: Beer/ Wine
SERVING: Lunch/ Dinner
Now this is the place to go if you want a REALLY good burger. One of the best in town. The food is really fresh and cooked to order. All the soups are home made. Really good service. $$

GREEK ISLANDS TAVERNA
3300 N Ocean Blvd., Fort Lauderdale: 954-565-5505
http://www.greekislandstaverna.com
CUISINE: Greek/ Mediterranean
DRINKS: Full Bar
SERVING: Lunch/ Dinner
Everything on the menu here is excellent. Specialties include the lamb chops, hummus and pita bread and grilled

octopus. The environment is typically Greek, loud and welcoming. $$$

INDIGO
Riverside Hotel
620 E. Las Olas Blvd., Fort Lauderdale: 954-467-0671
www.riversidehotel.com
CUISINE: Seafood/ American
DRINKS: Full Bar
SERVING: Breakfast/ Lunch/ Dinner
Located in the lobby of the historic **Riverside Hotel**, here you can dine and watch the endless parade of people that promenade along Las Olas Boulevard. Menu highlights include a char-grilled pork loin and a citrus crusted Florida grouper. $$-$$$

J. MARK'S RESTAURANT & BAR
1245 N Federal Hwy, Fort Lauderdale: 954-390-0770
http://www.jmarksrestaurant.com
CUISINE: American
DRINKS: Full Bar
SERVING: Lunch/ Dinner/ Brunch on weekends
Popular and upscale eatery, this place is usually busy and once you've had the food, you'll understand why. One of the best things on the menu: the Chilean Sea Bass that literally melts in your mouth. Crab cakes are also quite good. Very friendly staff. $$-$$$

KELLY'S LANDING
1305 SE 17th St., Ft Lauderdale: 954-760-7009
www.kellyslanding.com
CUISINE: American/ Seafood
DRINKS: Full Bar
SERVING: Lunch/ Dinner
Snowbirds searching for the flavors of home while visiting Florida will find what they're looking for at Kelly's Landing. They import lobsters daily from Boston and

serve up a popular New England-style seafood and clam chowder. $$

KURO
1 Seminole Way, Hollywood, 954-327-7625
www.seminolehardrockhollywood.com/fine-dining
CUISINE: Sushi/Japanese
DRINKS: Full bar
SERVING: Dinner; Lunch on Saturdays
PRICE RANGE: $$$
Spacious modern eatery set inside the Seminole Hard Rock Casino. Fresh sushi and unique crafted cocktails. Menu favorites: Tuna Crispy Rice and Wagyu Tacos.

LA BAMBA
4245 N Federal Hwy, Fort Lauderdale: 954-568-5662
http://www.labamba123.com
CUISINE: Mexican
DRINKS: Full Bar
SERVING: Lunch/ Dinner
If you know true Mexican food, you will know that this is standardized American-Mexican food. In other words, not very good. Service is adequate but the place can get really loud. $$

LAS VEGAS CUBAN CUISINE
2807 E Oakland Park Blvd., Fort Lauderdale: 954-564-1370
http://www.lasvegascubancuisine.com
CUISINE: Cuban
DRINKS: Full Bar
SERVING: Lunch/ Dinner
Very simple menu, all the Cuban basics. Good service and reasonable prices. Crowded for lunch. $$

LEMONGRASS ASIAN BISTRO

3811 N Federal Hwy, Fort Lauderdale: 954-564-4422
http://www.lemongrassasianbistro.com
CUISINE: Thai/ Sushi/ Vietnamese
DRINKS: Full Bar
SERVING: Lunch/ Dinner
Modern Asian bistro, the service is good and the food is
just a tad better than average. $$-$$$

LOUIE BOSSI'S RISTORANTE BAR PIZZERIA

1032 E Las Olas Blvd, Fort Lauderdale, 954-356-6699
www.louiebossi.com
CUISINE: Italian
DRINKS: Full Bar
SERVING: Lunch & Dinner
PRICE RANGE: $$
NEIGHBORHOOD: Downtown
Popular eatery serving authentic Italian cuisine including
Neapolitan pies, pastas, salami and piazza with bocce.
Happy hour every day. Creative cocktails like the
pineapple martini. Nice wine list. Indoor and outdoor
seating.

MAI-KAI POLYNESIAN DINNER SHOW

3599 N. Federal Hwy, Fort Lauderdale: 954-563-3272
http://www.maikai.com
ADMISSION: Show charge: $10.95 per person plus
dinner. Kids menu available.
The roaring drums mark the beginning of the exciting
"island revue." It's about as phony now as it was a
hundred years ago when they first came up with this
concept of a "romantic Hawaiian wedding dance" and the
"thrilling Samoan fire knife dance performed by our native
Polynesian dancers." To read it, you want to barf. But trust
me, it's a lot of fun. And the food's good, too.

MARIO'S CATALINA RESTAURANT

1611 N Federal Hwy, Fort Lauderdale: 954-563-4141
www.catalinarestaurant.net
CUISINE: Cuban/ Spanish
DRINKS: Beer/ Wine
SERVING: Lunch/ Dinner
Lively little restaurant with great beef empanadas and
Argentine style skirt steak. Another must-have is the
seafood-replete paella. The staff is warm and friendly. $$

MARKET 17
1850 SE 17th St., Fort Lauderdale: 954-835-5507
http://www.market17.net
CUISINE: American
DRINKS: Full Bar
SERVING: Dinner
With a fresh menu that changes daily, one of their more popular items is the charcuterie platter. They offer either a petite or a full portion on all their dishes. The wine list is good and reasonably priced. Another must try: the monkey bread. $$$

MOJO
4140 N Federal Hwy, Fort Lauderdale: 954-568-4443
http://www.mojofl.com
CUISINE: International
DRINKS: Full Bar
SERVING: Dinner
Good food being served up in a very colorful environment. The walls are covered with art. You won't be disappointed with anything on the menu, and the service is fast and friendly. Cool place with a good vibe. $$

PIZZA CITY
1509 E Las Olas Blvd., Fort Lauderdale: 954-522-2935
www.ats-a-pizza.com
CUISINE: Pizza
DRINKS: Beer/ Wine
SERVING: Lunch/ Dinner
Basic fare pizza, pasta, subs and calzones. They offer
gluten-free pizza crust. $$

RAINBOW PALACE
2787 E Oakland Park Blvd., Fort Lauderdale: 954-565-
5652
http://www.rainbowpalace.com
CUISINE: Chinese
DRINKS: Full Bar
SERVING: Lunch/ Dinner
Quite possibly the best Chinese food in Fort Lauderdale.
The ambiance is quite nice and the staff is friendly. The
menu is extensive. $$

RED COW
1025 N Federal Hwy, Ft Lauderdale, 954-652-1524
www.redcowftl.com
CUISINE: American (New) / Barbecue
DRINKS: Full Bar
SERVING: Lunch & Dinner, Sunday Brunch
PRICE RANGE: $$
A casual saloon (TVs play old Westerns) that serves BBQ
with a modern spin. Menu favorites include: Sweet potato
grits, BBQ ribs, brisket, pulled rotisserie chicken, smoked
turkey breast, skillet cornbread and smoked fish dip. The
meats are smoked on-site in a Mesquite brand cooker,
using cherry and hickey woods.

RUSTIC INN CRABHOUSE

4331 Anglers Ave., Fort Lauderdale: 954-584-1637
http://www.rusticinn.com
CUISINE: Seafood
DRINKS: Full Bar
SERVING: Lunch/ Dinner
Bright and raucous, in here you have the opportunity to take a mallet and crack your own crabs! Delicious as they are in their garlicky oil sauce, trust me, you will need the bibs they provide. On the water but in an odd location, this is not the place for a quiet, romantic dinner. Although entrees will run you between $10 - $20, crabs are market price, and they can get pricey. $$-$$$

SAGE FRENCH CAFÉ AND OYSTER BAR

2378 N. Federal Hwy., Ft. Lauderdale: 954-565-2299
http://www.sagecafe.net
CUISINE: French
DRINKS: Beer/ Wine
SERVING: Lunch/ Dinner
Superb country French cuisine at reasonable prices in a
casual French bistro setting. Among their best dishes is a
daube de boeuf (a slow cooked beef stew) and a *saumon
coulibiac* (salmon baked in a puff pastry). Their wine list
includes both French and domestic. $$

SEASONS 52

2428 E Sunrise Blvd. (inside Galleria Mall), Fort
Lauderdale: 954-537-1052
http://www.seasons52.com

E: American
KS: Full Bar
RVING: Lunch/ Dinner

While the décor here is somewhat dark and moody, it's always very lively. This place is great for an intimate dinner. The food is great and the service is also very good. You'll be surprised to know that everything on the menu is under 450 calories and they change it with the seasons. There's a HUGE bar, which is where I like to eat if I'm with just one other person. $$

SECRET GARDEN
THE PILLARS

111 N. Birch Rd., Fort Lauderdale: 954-467-9639
www.pillarshotel.com

This is the very nice restaurant in the posh and exclusive Pillars just off the Beach. They serve breakfast and lunch to hotel guests only, but at dinner they let members of the Secret Garden Society in. Chef Hammi combines fresh food with interesting cross-cultural ingredients and elegant presentations. His clean and bright flavors reflect the influences of a Moroccan heritage and techniques absorbed while working under top chefs in some of New York City's greatest kitchens. (Call or email them at secretgarden@ pillarshotel.com to see if they'll let you squeeze in for dinner.)

SUBLIME
1431 N Federal Hwy, Fort Lauderdale: 954-615-1431
http://www.sublimerestaurant.com
CUISINE: American/ Vegan
DRINKS: Full Bar
SERVING: Dinner
Who says vegan food is not tasty? Although this is not the best vegan food, it's still not bad. Desserts are especially good. The atmosphere is nice and the staff is friendly. $$$

SWEET NECTAR CHARCOAL GRILL AND SPIRITS
1017 E Las Olas Blvd, Ft Lauderdale, 954-761-2122
www.sweetnectarbuzz.com
CUISINE: American (New) / Tapas / Small Plates
DRINKS: Full Bar
SERVING: Lunch & Dinner
PRICE RANGE: $$
Casual neighborhood spot with a menu of American small plates. A favorite of locals who keep coming back for the classic cuisine and handcrafted cocktails. (At happy hour, those expensive craft cocktails cost 50% less.) Only 30 people can squeeze into the interior, but they can handle about 100 outside, so if it's summer, make sure you're inside. The whole snapper is char-grilled, so that's the best option. The Brussels sprouts are roasted in a skillet and topped with a kimchi vinaigrette that gives them a pleasant bite.

TIMPANO

450 E Las Olas Blvd., Fort Lauderdale: 954-462-9119
http://www.timpanochophouse.net
CUISINE: Steakhouse/ Italian
DRINKS: Full Bar
SERVING: Lunch/ Dinner
Stylish and trendy, there are always pretty people in this
place. A must have is their Black Skillet Mussels. But the
steaks are as good as the pasta dishes. $$

WILD SEA OYSTER BAR & GRILLE

620 E Las Olas Blvd, Fort Lauderdale, 954-467-2555
www.wildsealasolas.com
CUISINE: Seafood/Steakhouse
DRINKS: Full bar
SERVING: Dinner nightly
PRICE RANGE: $$$
Upscale seafood eatery specializing in fresh oysters. Menu
favorites: Crab cakes and Po' Boy Sliders. Great selection
of wines.

AGAVE TACO BAR
2949 N. Federal Hwy, Ste 3, Ft Lauderdale, 954-530-9065
www.agave-tacobar.com
CUISINE: Mexican
DRINKS: Beer & Wine
SERVING: Lunch/Dinner
PRICE RANGE: $$
A modern Mexican Taqueria serving up designer tacos
and other authentic Mexican fare. They have a good
deal on Taco Tuesdays. You can choose from 15 fillings
(like pork, chicken, carne asada, beef, veggie, picadillo,
pork belly, shrimp, and more). Menu includes creative
dessert popsicles with flavors like Strawberry filled with
condensed milk.

ANTHONY'S COAL FIRED PIZZA
2203 S Federal Hwy, Fort Lauderdale: 954-462-5555
http://anthonyscoalfiredpizza.com
CUISINE: Pizza/ Italian
DRINKS: Beer/ Wine
SERVING: Lunch/ Dinner

Just really good pizza. You'll love the slightly blackened crust. Also good here are the chicken wings but for those seeking more traditional Italian dishes, they also have a selection of pasta dishes that are sure to please. $

BETTY'S SOUL FOOD RESTAURANT
601 NW 22nd Rd., Fort Lauderdale: 954-583-9121
http://www.allmenus.com/fl/fort-lauderdale/15970-bettys-soul-food-restaurant/menu/
CUISINE: Southern Soul Food
DRINKS: No Alcohol
SERVING: Breakfast/ Lunch/ Dinner
This is the place to get Southern soul food. The menu is not too reliable so ask the waiter what the chef has going on. Typical items being served up: pig tails, catfish, fried chicken, chitlins, oxtail and collard greens. Always a mix of people here. $

BOMBAY CAFE

3060 N Andrews Ave., Wilton Manors: 954-568-0600
http://www.bombay-cafe.com
CUISINE: Indian
DRINKS: Beer/ Wine
SERVING: Lunch/ Dinner
Best Indian food in Broward County. The place doesn't
look like much, but who cares? When you're having this
kind of great food, nothing else matters. They have a great
Wednesday night buffet. $

CASA FRIDA

5441 N Federal Hwy, Ft Lauderdale, 954-530-3668
www.casafridamexicancuisine.com
CUISINE: Mexican / Spanish
DRINKS: Beer & Wine only
SERVING: Lunch & Dinner; closed Mon
PRICE RANGE: $$
Inspired by the famous painter – Frida Kahlo, this
colorful eatery features cuisine from a variety of regions
of Mexico, all homemade and inspired by the recipes of
the owners' ancestors. On the menu is a line that reads,
"There's Mexican food and there's the food of Mexico."
This place serves the latter, so don't expect to come here to
eat a chimichanga. LOL. Chiles rellenos, enchiladas Frida
(stuffed with chicken and roasted tomatillo sauce on top)
and a slow-roasted pork dish, Cochinita Pibil, which is
marinated in achiote citrus juice, are good bets.

EGG N YOU DINER
2621 N Federal Hwy, Fort Lauderdale: 954-564-2045
CUISINE: American/ Diner
DRINKS: No Alcohol
SERVING: Breakfast/ Lunch
Typical greasy spoon that doesn't disappoint. Service may
be a little slow and there is usually a wait for breakfast on
the weekends. $

THE FLORIDIAN RESTAURANT
1410 E. Las Olas Blvd., Fort Lauderdale: 954-463-4041
www.thefloridiandiner.com
CUISINE: American/ Diner
DRINKS: Beer/ Wine
SERVING: Open 24 hours
This greasy spoon has been around for many years, 63 to
be precise. A favorite among locals, this place is packed
during the weekend. Great place for breakfast serving up
oversized omelets, hot oatmeal, and biscuits and gravy. $

FRESH FIRST
1637 SE 17th St, Ft Lauderdale, 954-763-3344
www.freshfirst.com
CUISINE: Gluten-free / Smoothies
DRINKS: Beer & Wine Only (even the beer and wine are
gluten-free)
SERVING: Breakfast & Lunch; closed Sun

PRICE RANGE: $$

South Florida's first 100% gluten-free eatery and juicery serving a creative menu using fresh ingredients and superfoods. Great spot for a healthy breakfast or lunch. There are 3 excellent burgers: portabello, raw lentil and quinoa veggie. Or get for one of their creative and tasty bowls; zucchini puttanesca (with garbanzo beans, lentils, red peppers, scallions, Kalamata olives, basil in a garlic-lemon sauce); or the bowl with veggie fried quinoa (with scallions, red peppers, carrots, purple cabbage and a fried egg on top).

JACK'S OLD FASHION HAMBURGER HOUSE

4201 N Federal Hwy, Fort Lauderdale: 954-565-9960

www.jacksoldfashionhamburgers.com

CUISINE: American

DRINKS: No Alcohol

SERVING: Lunch/ Dinner

This is the place to go if you want a no frills, basic hamburger or cheeseburger. They do charge you extra for lettuce and tomato. They also have hot dogs and a few sandwiches. $

LA SPADA'S ORIGINAL HOAGIES
233-B East Commercial Blvd, Lauderdale-by-the-Sea: 954-776-7893
http://www.laspadashoagies.com
CUISINE: Sandwiches
DRINKS: No Alcohol
SERVING: Lunch/ Dinner
Whether you call it a sub or a hoagie, this place has the best around. Fresh meats and veggies piled high on fresh bread makes them simply delicious! $

LE PATIO
2401 NE 11th Ave., Wilton Manors: 954-530-4641
http://www.lepatiowiltonmanors.com
CUISINE: International/ Comfort Foods
DRINKS: Beer/ Wine
SERVING: Lunch/ Dinner
YIKES! What a great place this is. You definitely want to sit in the back patio. It's a very cute and charming bistro atmosphere. The food is absolutely stupendous. Favorites include the French Onion soup and the homemade lasagna. $

LESTER'S DINER
250 W State Road 84, Fort Lauderdale: 954-525-5641
CUISINE: American Diner
DRINKS: Beer/ Wine
SERVING: Breakfast/ Lunch/ Dinner
Typical American diner, you will absolutely love this place. Sit at the bar or sit in a booth, the wait staff will take very good care of you. All the typical dishes you will find here and the desserts are decadent. $

PIRATE REPUBLIC SEAFOOD & GRILL
400 SW 3rd Ave, Fort Lauderdale, 954-761-3500
www.piraterepublicbar.com
CUISINE: Seafood / Brazilian
DRINKS: Full bar
SERVING: Lunch/Dinner
PRICE RANGE: $$
Waterfront restaurant on the river with a pirate theme.
Menu picks: Fresh oysters, coconut shrimp, whole fried
snapper, shrimp Alfredo. There are some nice dishes you
won't see just anywhere—the Pirate Bowl (with clams,
calamari, shrimp, mussels in a broth full of flavors from
garlic, butter and white wine) and Brazilian seafood
moqueca (a mix of lobster and octopus in a great sauce).
Great view from the deck. Their Key Lime Pie is a must.

PIZZACRAFT ARTISAN PIZZERIA
330 Himmarshee St Ste 101, Fort Lauderdale, 954-616-
8028
www.pizzacraftpizzeria.com
CUISINE: Pizza/Italian
DRINKS: Full bar
SERVING: Lunch & Dinner
PRICE RANGE: $$

Creative menu of pizza and typical Italian fare. Here you'll be treated to wood fired pizzas (meatball pizza is a favorite). Don't overlook the variety of house made pastas. Half-price specials on Wednesdays. Nice bar selection.

PRESS GOURMET SANDWICHES
6206 N Federal Hwy, Fort Lauderdale, 954-440-0422
www.pressgourmetsandwiches.com
CUISINE: Sandwiches
DRINKS: No Booze
SERVING: Lunch & Dinner
PRICE RANGE: $
NEIGHBORHOOD: East side of US 1
Basically a sandwich shop (with a clever newspaper theme) serving gourmet sandwiches and sides like Truffle Fries and Mac'n Cheese Balls. A couple of culinary stars that had a food truck decided to open a permanent location, and this is it. Simply wonderful food prepared with top-notch ingredients (that you'd expect from graduates of the culinary school Johnson & Wales) and the portions are huge. The "Sentinel" is a cheesesteak sandwich with caramelized onions that melts in your mouth. The "Journal" is a pork lover's delight—pulled pork delectably flavored with a sweet tangy BBQ sauce, coleslaw and onion straws that are crispy and delightful. (You can order the onion straws on the side, which I definitely recommend—you will want more of them.) Order and pay at the counter. Weekly specials.

RIVERSIDE MARKET SOUTH
3218 SE 6th Ave, Fort Lauderdale, 954-524-8986
www.theriversidemarket.com
CUISINE: Gastropub
DRINKS: Beer & Wine Only
SERVING: Lunch & Dinner; Closed Sun
PRICE RANGE: $$
NEIGHBORHOOD: Btwn the Sailboat Bend and

Riverside Park

Great selection of food including their famous flat bread pizzas. Menu picks: Shrimp Po Boy, pulled pork sandwich, mahi tacos, turkey meatball sliders and pork tacos. The desserts from nearby Pies in a Jar are worth your attention—served in chilled mason jars, you can get things like Key Lime Goodness, Chocolate Mousse Pie and other really nice selections. What's really impressive is the 32 cutting edge craft draft lines and a selection of 350 bottled beers. I'm always suspicious of places that carry hundreds of varieties of bottled beer. Beer ought to be fresh and you wonder how long that quaint beer from Lithuania has been sitting in the cooler. A year? Two years. Try out some of the local beers produced in florida, like J. Wakefield in Miami, Funky Buddha Brewery in Oakland Park.

SMOKE BBQ
3351 NE 32nd St, Fort Lauderdale, 954-530-5334
www.eatbbqnow.com
CUISINE: BBQ
DRINKS: Full bar
SERVING: Lunch & Dinner; closed Monday

PRICE RANGE: $$
Authentic BBQ eatery with a varied menu. Menu favorites
include: Brisket, Ribs, and Pulled Pork.

SOUTHPORT RAW BAR
1536 Cordova Rd, Ft Lauderdale, 954-525-2526
www.southportrawbar.com
CUISINE: Seafood
DRINKS: Beer & Wine
SERVING: Lunch/Dinner/Late Night
PRICE RANGE: $$
Great meeting place in business for over 40 years that's a
mixture of dive bar and boat dock eatery. Great to sit out
here and scarf down shellfish while looking at the water.
Menu picks: Fresh raw oysters, Fried Clam strips, dolphin,
excellent clam chowder and the very best conch chowder
you can find in these parts. Good selection of beers. Indoor
and outdoor seating.

TACOCRAFT TAQUERIA & TEQUILA BAR
204 SW 2nd St, Fort Lauderdale, 954-463-2003
www.tacocraft.com
CUISINE: Mexican
DRINKS: Full bar
SERVING: Lunch/Dinner/Late Night
PRICE RANGE: $$
This place is a locals' favorite – especially Taco Tuesday
when the tacos are cheap. And they don't limit your choice
of the kind of taco you can order on Tuesday. You can
order any taco on the menu and still get the low Tuesday
price. The tacos are made fresh daily here in the store.
Menu favorites: Short rib taco, chicken taco, blackened ahi
tuna. Indoor and outdoor seating, late night and after work
crowds.

TOP HAT DELICATESSEN
415 NE 3rd St, Fort Lauderdale, 954-900-3896
www.tophatftl.com
CUISINE: Deli
DRINKS: Full bar
SERVING: Breakfast & Lunch
PRICE RANGE: $$
Modern twist on a New York Deli feature traditional deli
fare like cheese blintzes, lox, sandwiches and non-deli
items like ramen and crafted cocktails. Menu favorites
include: Noodle Kugel and Rueben Egg Rolls. Crafted
cocktails and beer.

TREASURE TROVE
2933 SE 5th St, Fort Lauderdale, 954-522-8385
CUISINE: American (traditional)
SERVING: Lunch/Dinner/Late Night
PRICE RANGE: $
You can overlook the silly pirate theme at this place on
the beach that has a reputation as a bar but the food should
not be ignored. Menu picks: Conch fritters and "Andre's
Famous Jerk Wings." Popular with locals is the rum punch
and the Mahi tacos. The food is cheap, but it's still very
good. On Taco Tuesdays they offer ultra-cheap chicken or
beef tacos all day. Huge array of hot sauces.

TARKS OF DANIA BEACH

1317 S Federal Hwy, Dania Beach, 954-925-8275
No Website
CUISINE: Sandwiches/Bar Grub
DRINKS: Full bar
SERVING: Lunch/Dinner/Late Night
PRICE RANGE: $

Dive bar with a menu of tasty eats. I've been driving up to little Dania to get the chicken wings and the steamer clams here for three decades. They're just as good today as they were then. Favorites: Conch salad and Grilled grouper sandwich. Very busy place – no reservations. Counter service plus a few tables outside. Since 1966.

WARSAW COFFEE COMPANY

815 NE 13th St, Fort Lauderdale, 954-990-4189
www.warsawcoffee.com
CUISINE: American/Diner
DRINKS: Beer & Wine Only
SERVING: Breakfast, Lunch & Dinner
PRICE RANGE: $

Coffee shop with an extensive menu. Great smoothies,
coffees. Nice selection of pastries and sweets. Try
famous kitchen sink cookies.

TARPON BEND
200 SW 2nd St., Fort Lauderdale: 954-523-3233
http://www.tarponbend.com/index-54854.php.html
CUISINE: Seafood
DRINKS: Full Bar
SERVING: Lunch/ Dinner
This place has incredibly fresh seafood, the oysters are
shucked to order. Try their specialty, smoked fish dip. $

JRTS BAR & GRILL
Fort Lauderdale, 954-900-5584
antation.com

5 plasma HD TVs along with 2 of South
.t HD TVs. They play every sport, every
ga. ent. Stop by for you watch TV.) Daily drink
specials. . ate parties, catering available.
lunch, dinner or just a drink and meet Kim Bokamper.
Boxing, UFC, basketball, soccer, hockey, baseball, special
events. (They have a Game Room where your kids can
play.)

FLANIGAN'S
1479 E. Commercial Blvd., Oakland Park: 954-493-5329
www.flanigans.net
The atmosphere of the restaurant is fun, they have lively
music and everyone seems to enjoy it. The pina colada is
one of the best around, not too sweet and you can actually
taste the alcohol. I grew up eating his baby back ribs.

LANDLUBBERS RAW BAR & GRILL
1851 N. Pine Island Rd., Plantation: 954-473-2884
www.landlubbersrawbar.com
Out west of Fort Lauderdale, you'll find this friendly sports
bar. This place serves up big fat burgers and fresh seafood.
Crab cakes which were made with a very generous
portion of real lump crab meat and the burgers are well
above average. All the waitresses and waiters are nice and
pleasant. (I focus on the raw bar. Here you can get a dozen
oysters, raw or steamed, for $11. On South Beach where
I live, those very same oysters will run you $3.50 to $4
each.)

MCSORLEY'S BEACH PUB

837 N. Fort Lauderdale Beach Blvd., Fort Lauderdale:
954-565-4446

mcsorleysbeachpub.com

With 25 TVs you can watch any sporting event you want.
Just a great place to drink some suds and watch the world
turn. I love the rooftop bar with its killer view of the
ocean. If there are no sports on TV, you will find this place
transformed into a cool young hangout with great music
and a great ladies' night on a Wednesday.

MILLER'S ALE HOUSE

2861 N. Federal Hwy, Fort Lauderdale: 954-565-5747
www.millersalehouse.com

Very good place to watch sports in Ft lauderdale. Central
location, free parking, very good service, reasonable prices,
tasty food and lots of TVs everywhere to catch a game.
The Ale House is a decent sports bar with a good selection
of beers, a good menu, and some great food and drink
specials during the week. (It's hard to beat the $9.95 Prime
Rib or 35 Fried Shrimp on Thursdays.)

SLACKERS BAR & GRILL
995 State Road 84, Fort Lauderdale: 954-530-4758
www.slackersbarandgrill.com
They have 33 TVs to watch your favorite game on. They
even offer customers who get a table near the wall their
own TV to watch whatever you like. Hell, you can even
have a remote and change your own channel. They show
all NFL football games with Direc TV's Sunday Ticket, all
MLB, NBA, NHL and Rugby, and also show all UFC pay-
per-view events and every Sunday they throw a NASCAR
party. They have recently added the College Football
package and the Big Ten Network.

STOUT BAR & GRILL
3419 N. Andrews Ave., Oakland Park: 754-223-5678
www.stoutsportsbarandgrill.com
Golf, soccer, rugby, you name it, they show it. They have
32 HDTV screens to watch while you chow down on
their traditional menu featuring some Irish favorites. They
have a flatbread with corned beef, Swiss cheese and grain
mustard that's really good. $8.

QUARTERDECK

1541 Cordova Rd., Fort Lauderdale: 954-524-6163
2933 E. Las Olas Blvd., Fort Lauderdale Beach: 954-525-2010
quarterdeckrestaurants.com

A neighborhood bar with solid food, ice-cold beer, good drinks, fair prices. Seafood, steaks and ribs, burgers, wings, the usual menu for this kind of place.

Chapter 4
NIGHTLIFE

THE CULTURE ROOM
3045 N. Federal Hwy, Fort Lauderdale: 954-564-1074
http://www.cultureroom.net
If you consider rock and heavy metal to be culture, visit the Culture Room and bang your head to local bands. Open nightly from 8pm to 3am.

DICEY RILEY'S
217 SW 2nd St., Fort Lauderdale: 954-522-1908
No web site
A downtown favorite for those who love a rowdy Irish bar featuring some of the best cover bands in Fort Lauderdale. Be prepared to stand very close to the person next to you

on the weekends and feel free to join the crowd as they attempt to sing along with the band. 21+ only.

BLONDIE'S SPORTS BAR

229 S Fort Lauderdale Beach Blvd, Fort Lauderdale: 954-728-9801

http://itsbetteronthebeach.com/blondies/

Serving up the "World's Longest Happy Hour (noon-10pm) Dirty Blondes Sports Bar is a favorite amongst locals and voted 'Best Bar to Take Out-Of-Towners' by New Times Magazine. Whether you're looking to take in the game day action on one of 50 flat screen TVs, soak in the sun and scenery with a bucket of beer and a burger, add a little air hockey or pop-a-shot competition to a night out with friends, or use pinball and pool as an icebreaker for a first date, Dirty Blondes casual rock-n-roll atmosphere has a little something for everyone.

EBAR / CLUB BAR 13
215 SW 2nd St., Fort Lauderdale: 305-928-3227
Fort Lauderdale's only premier Latin nightclub - Salsa,
Merengue, Bachata and Reggaeton mixed with freestyle
Americano. Underground dance party in (2) dark RED
DISTRICT tunnels - industrial and urban design.

ELBO ROOM
241 S. Fort Lauderdale Blvd, Fort Lauderdale 954-463-
4615
http://www.elboroom.com
Formerly Spring Break central, the Elbo Room has actually
managed to maintain its rowdy and divey reputation
by serving up frequent drink specials and live bands.
Ironically, it was almost torn down until the Penrod family
of chic and sleek Nikki Beach fame bought the place to
keep it alive. No matter what, it'll always be a beloved
dive. Open daily from 10am to 2am.

EXIT 66
219 S. Fort Lauderdale Beach Blvd., Fort Lauderdale: 954-
357-9981
http://m.exit66fl.com
Pool Party: open every weekend from 1pm until dark.
Located 1/2 block North of Las Olas Blvd and A1A.

O LOUNGE
333 E. Las Olas Blvd., Fort Lauderdale: 954-523-1000
www.yolorestaurant.com
From happy hour habitués to night owls, O-lounge
provides a unique vibe in a polished setting that glows as
the night progresses. It's a comfortable gathering spot that
feels trendy but without being pretentious. Here you can
people watch, talk with friends and enjoy DJs mixing and
blending funk, lounge and retro music.

ORIGINAL FAT CAT'S

320 Himmarshee St., Fort Lauderdale: 954-467-5867
They have a Facebook page
Popular downtown dive bar rocking out to live local bands
every night. Great place for those who need a break from
the booty music found in most other clubs. Widest Craft
Beer selection in all of Broward. Happy Hour 5pm-10pm
and live entertainment daily. 21+ only.

THE PARROT

911 Sunrise Lane, Fort Lauderdale: 954-563-1493
http://www.parrotlounge.com
Fort Lauderdale's most famous dive bar, The Parrot is a
local's and out-of-towner's choice for an evening of beer
(16 kinds on tap), bonding, and browsing the bar's gallery
of photos of almost everyone who's ever imbibed here
since its opening in 1970. Open Sunday through Thursday
from 11am to 2am, and Friday and Saturday from 11am to
3am.

THE POOR HOUSE

110 SW 3rd Ave., Fort Lauderdale: 954-522-5145
http://www.poorhousebar.com
There's nothing poor about this microbrew hangout, where
excellent live music by local bands starts at midnight and

goes on well into the wee hours. A friendly, lively, mixed crowd composes a generational cross section where the gap is bridged by a common love of music, cold beer, and good times. Open nightly from 6pm-4am.

POSH LOUNGE
110 N. Federal Hwy, Fort Lauderdale: 954-763-3553
http://www.poshlasolas.com
Posh Lounge incorporates contemporary decor with an extensive wine list, Mediterranean tapas, hookahs and a resident DJ to create a unique and stylish atmosphere.

REVOLUTION LIVE
100 Nugent Ave., Fort Lauderdale: 954-449-1025
www.jointherevolution.net
Some of today's hottest indie bands play here, but if you're not into live music, fret not because this cavernous place is a dance club, too. Open Thursday to Sunday until 4am. Opening hours and cover charges vary, depending on what band is playing.

RHYTHM & VINE
401 NE 5th Terrace, Fort Lauderdale, 954-533-3734
www.rhythm-vine.com
Dance Club featuring a little beer garden with rotating food trucks. Live DJ. Food menu features comfort food bites like BBQ & Mac and cheese. Closed Mon & Tues.

ROCK BAR
219 S Fort Lauderdale Beach Blvd., Fort Lauderdale: 954-728-9804
www.itsbetteronthebeach.com/rock-bar
When you want to pick up the energy and turn up the volume step up to Rock Bar. This rockin' beach bar offers a typical American menu and an oceanfront setting. 2-for-1 margaritas and drink specials daily. If you don't feel like leaving after your meal, Rock Bar also offers a hookah menu and live entertainment on the weekends.

ROUND UP COUNTRY WESTERN BAR
9020 W State Rd. 84, Davie: 954-423-1990
http://www.roundupnightclub.com
Known world wide for its country western dancing (Two Step, Line Dance, Cha Cha, East Coast Swing, West Coast Swing), and live entertainment. Full service restaurant with a full dinner menu.

SEMINOLE HARD ROCK HOTEL & CASINO
1 Seminole Way, Hollywood: 866-502-7529
http://www.seminolehardrockhollywood.com
When it comes to nightlife in these parts, some of the hottest lounges and clubs are located within this mega-complex. Among them, Pangaea and Gryphon, opened by a NYC nightlife impresario, and Opium, which -- gasp -- crossed the county line from Miami and was followed by its faithful disciples of A-listers and club kids spanning the tricounty area. Also here: popular dance club Passion, Murphy's Law Irish Pub, Automatic Slim's, and more.

SHO NIGHTCLUB
15 W Las Olas Blvd., Fort Lauderdale: 954-462-3322
Mixing a state-of-the-art sound system and over-the-top décor bringing partygoers into a sleek and stylish atmosphere. The legendary nightlife location brings a high-energy decadent atmosphere complete with outstanding sound. Music appeals to all patrons, with a mix of house, hip-hop and open format. Open four nights a week, Thurs–Sat, 9pm to 4am. Thursday nights, guests can enjoy open format for the Electric Karma Party. Fridays will include House and Saturday's guests can enjoy the best open format sets in town. SHO will also be opening the second level of its club for Industry Tuesdays.

SHOOTERS

3033 NE 32nd Ave, Fort Lauderdale: 954-566-2855
www.shooterswaterfront.com

This waterfront bar is quintessential Fort Lauderdale. Inside you'll find nautical types, families, and young professionals mixed with a good dose of sunburned tourists enjoying the live reggae, jazz, or Jimmy Buffett-style tunes, with the gorgeous backdrop of the bay and marinas all around. Open Monday through Friday from 11:30am to 2am, Saturday from 11:30am to 3am, and Sunday from 10am to 2am.

VIBE LAS OLAS

301 Las Olas Blvd., Fort Lauderdale: 954-713-7313
http://www.vibelasolas.com

A modern and sleek mixed with natural elements club, with a signature lighting display inside and out that puts an exclamation point on this corner of lower Las Olas Boulevard.

WRECK BAR
B Ocean

1140 Seabreeze Blvd., Fort Lauderdale: 954-524-5551
Reconnect in the unique Wreck Bar, an iconic favorite for decades serving cocktails and light fare. Open daily from 5:30pm-12:00am. Live mermaid show at the iconic Wreck Bar every Friday at 6pm, bring the kids, this kind of show is perfect for someone young.

Chapter 5
ATTRACTIONS

AQUATIC ADVENTURES BOAT RENTAL
301 Seabreeze Blvd., Ft Lauderdale, 954-459-8020
www.aquaticboatrental.com
FEES: Costs based on what you do. They offer kite
surfing, kayaking, parasailing or you can rent one of their
powerboats. They operate trips and tours by the hour,
half day and full day with all the water sports equipment
included. The service also provides free transportation to
and from area hotels. There's a kite surfing school here.

BILLIE SWAMP SAFARI

30000 Gator Tail Trl., Clewiston, 863-983-6101
www.billieswamp.com/
ADMISSION: fee varies
This is an up-close-and-personal look into the Seminole
reservation. Daily tours into the wetlands and hardwood
hammocks where you can see deer, water buffalo, bison,
wild hogs, ornery ostriches, rare birds, and alligators in
their natural habitat. You can also stay overnight in a native
Tiki hut for $35 per night.

BONNET HOUSE

900 N. Birch Rd., Fort Lauderdale: 954-563-5393
http://www.bonnethouse.org
ADMISSION: fee varies
Historic 35-acre plantation home and estate. You can only
go through it with a guided tour, however, you might want
to ask about the love story associated with this place.
Beautiful grounds, whimsical artwork and interesting
design.

BUTTERFLY WORLD
3600 W. Sample Rd., Ft. Lauderdale: 954-977-4400
http://www.butterflyworld.com
ADMISSION: $25 adults and seniors, $20 children ages
3-11.
Everything Butterfly. Kids especially love the Bug
Museum which allows them to interact with little critters,
with the assistance of well trained employees.

FORT LAUDERDALE ANTIQUE CAR MUSEUM
1527 S.W. 1st Ave., Fort Lauderdale: 954-779-7300
http://www.antiquecarmuseum.org
ADMISSION: fee varies
Boy, will you be surprised at what you'll see inside. They
have a very nice collection of automobiles, including many
Packards, from limousines to speedsters. Photography is
allowed.

FORT LAUDERDALE SUN TROLLEY
290 NE 3rd Av, Fort Lauderdale: 954-761-3543
http://www.suntrolley.com
Small fee
This is a great way to get around downtown Fort

Lauderdale and the beaches. It's convenient and inexpensive. They also offer an all day pass for $2. Can't beat that.

GONDOLAS WEST

Bahia Mar Yachting Center, 801 Seabreeze Blvd, Ft Lauderdale, 954-609-6674

www.gondolaswest.com

A lot of people know that Lauderdale calls itself the "American Venice," but very few of them have actually gotten into a boat to tour a few of the 165 miles of inland waterways that chop up this city. You'll see some of the loveliest (and most expensive) real estate in the country from a seat in these silent electric boats trimmed with teak carrying a maximum of six passengers, these boats get you into waterways and canals the larger tourist boats can't reach. View the beautiful canals of Ft. Lauderdale and nature's beauty behind some quite majestic homes. Variety of tours available including historic and eco tours.

GULFSTREAM PARK RACING & CASINO

901 South Federal Hwy, Hallandale Beach: 954-454-7000

http://www.gulfstreampark.com

Admission: Free to the park.

South Florida's premier thoroughbred racetrack, home of the foremost Triple Crown prep races including the Florida Derby. The nation's finest 3-year old thoroughbreds, jockeys and trainers spend their winter at Gulfstream Park. Slots, poker and other casino action spread out over two casino floors, adjacent to the historic Gulfstream Park racetrack. Open 365 days a year; 850 slot machines, electronic table games and hi-stakes poker.

HILLSBORO INLET LIGHTHOUSE

Hillsboro Inlet, off A1A, Hillsboro Beach: 954-781-1817

http://www.hillsborolighthouse.org

ADMISSION: fee varies

Standing 136 feet above water, this lighthouse marks the

northern end of the Florida Reef. It contains a
5,500,000-candlepower light and is the most powerful
light on the East Coast of the United States. There's
an interesting story attached to this landmark, the
disappearance of barefoot mailman James Hamilton, which
to this day remains a mystery.

HUGH TAYLOR BIRCH STATE PARK
3109 E. Sunrise Blvd., Fort Lauderdale: 954-564-4521
www.floridastateparks.org/park/Hugh-Taylor-Birch
ADMISSION: fee varies
Picnicking, camping, bike rental, swimming and canoeing
smack dab in the middle of the city. This 180-acre park
offers a calming getaway from the hustle and bustle of the
city. The value of this resource to Fort Lauderdale can't be
overestimated. I used to drive by it year after year until I
took my first step inside. The fact that it was preserved and
not developed is the biggest surprise. But here you'll get a
feeling what the area looked like to early settlers.

INTERNATIONAL SWIMMING HALL OF FAME

1 Hall of Fame Dr., Fort Lauderdale: 954-462-6536

http://www.ishof.org

ADMISSION: fee varies

The museum houses the world's largest collection of water-related memorabilia and in the store, you will find anything and everything related to the aquatic sport. One of the best spots in Fort Lauderdale to get the kind of souvenirs you really won't find anywhere else.

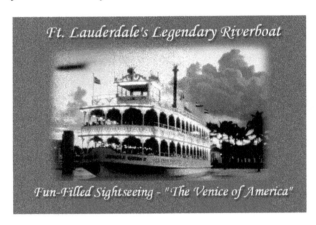

JUNGLE QUEEN RIVERBOAT

Bahia Mar Boating Center, 801 Seabreeze Blvd., Fort Lauderdale: 954-462-5596

http://www.junglequeen.com

ADMISSION: check web site

Cruise along the waterways of Fort Lauderdale as you enjoy a BBQ dinner and show onboard this old world riverboat. This old boat has been plying the waterways here for decades, and it's the ultimate touristy thing to do in Fort Lauderdale, but just get over it and go do it. It's not nearly as touristy as the Duck Tour! And here, you get a decent meal while you tour the waterways. To come to Fort Lauderdale and not see the waterways is to miss one of the great things about the town. It's just a matter of how you want to experience it: hire a private boat, go on the Duck Tour, do the Jungle Queen.

LADY HELEN FISHING CHARTERS
1534 SE 15th St. #3, Fort Lauderdale: 954-336-3256
http://www.ladyhelencharters.com
FEES: check web site
Private fishing charters for up to 4 anglers on the 29' twin diesel sport fisherman the "Lady Helen." Children are welcome and encouraged to participate. Full safety equipment. Many years ago, South Florida used to be a fisherman's heaven. But the business is no longer as vital as it used to be. With the dearth of charter fishing boats, one wonders about the "sustainable fish" you read about on pompous menus in fancy restaurants. Whenever I go on one of these trips, I always release the fish after it's caught.

LAS OLAS BOULEVARD
Fort Lauderdale
Very popular and quaint street located in downtown Fort Lauderdale. Here you will find good food and good shopping, along a few historical points of interest. Shopping includes boutiques, art galleries and antique stores.

LAS OLAS RIVERFRONT
Andrews Ave. at SE 2nd St., Fort Lauderdale
This was once a very nice place to spend an afternoon and evening. It is now a mere shadow of its former self and maybe not even that good. Only one decent restaurant still exists, the **Briney Pub**. You can pick up the water taxi there which is nice and there is a very good river cruise boat, but that's about it. In the evening, it is a hangout for rude kids and panhandlers.

MAI-KAI POLYNESIAN DINNER SHOW

3599 N Federal Hwy, Fort Lauderdale: 954-563-3272
http://www.maikai.com
ADMISSION: there's a fee for the show
The roaring drums mark the beginning of the exciting
"island revue." It's about as phony now as it was a
hundred years ago when they first came up with this
concept of a "romantic Hawaiian wedding dance" and the
"thrilling Samoan fire knife dance performed by our native
Polynesian dancers." To read it, you want to barf. But trust
me, it's a lot of fun. And the food's good, too.

MCGINNIS WATERSKI

2421 SW 46 Ave., Fort Lauderdale: 954-214-2792
www.mcski.com
FEES: Beginner lesson: fee varies
This place is really great and teaches those who want to
learn as well as help to improve the skills of those who
already know how to ski. Call to reserve.

MUSEUM OF DISCOVERY & SCIENCE

401 SW 2nd St., Fort Lauderdale: 954-467-6637
http://www.mods.org
ADMISSION: fee varies
Although the museum is geared towards children, adults
won't feel like they're in a kiddie museum. The IMAX
theatre is really something to experience.

NSU ART MUSEUM

1 E. Las Olas Blvd., Fort Lauderdale: 954-525-5500
www.nsuartmuseum.org
ADMISSION: fee varies
With more than 200 paintings; 50 sculptures and1,200
works on paper, this is truly a fantastic modern-art
facility. They also showcase more than 90 Cuban
artists in exile around the world. With traveling
exhibits and continuing art classes, the museum offers
free admission from 5 to 8pm on the third Thursday of
every month.

OLD DILLARD CULTURAL ARTS MUSEUM

1009 NW 4th St., Fort Lauderdale: 754-322-8828
www.broward.k12.fl.us/olddillardmuseum/home/index.
html
ADMISSION: fee varies
Include a visit to Fort Lauderdale's historic African
American museum -- it is one you will not want to miss.
The Old Dillard Museum is a cultural and educational
center that was originally Old Dillard High School. Built in
1924 as the first school for blacks in Fort Lauderdale, this
landmark was restored and exists today because of broad
community efforts.

OLD FORT LAUDERDALE VILLAGE & MUSEUM

219 SW Second Ave., Fort Lauderdale: 954-463-4431
http://www.fortlauderdalehistorycenter.org
ADMISSION: fee varies
This is a terrific place to go whether you're a tourist or
a local. This place is rich with the fun history of Fort
Lauderdale. Great for history buffs.

STRANAHAN HOUSE

335 SE 6th Ave., Fort Lauderdale: 954-524-4736
http://www.stranahanhouse.org
ADMISSION fee varies
A worthwhile little museum of South Florida pioneer
life, this is Fort Lauderdale's oldest standing structure.
It is filled with turn-of-the-20th-century furnishings and
historical photos of the area.

WATER TAXI

All over Fort Lauderdale: 954-467-6677
http://www.watertaxi.com/watertaxi/fort-lauderdale
ADMISSION: fee varies
Unlimited rides all day in Fort Lauderdale and Hollywood.
MOONLIGHT MADNESS – After 5pm $10. (Must be
purchased on board after 5pm)
This is a particularly nice way to get around the main hub

of Fort Lauderdale. You get a very different perspective of this town from its waterways that snake through its beautiful neighborhoods with a great view of the city's most beautiful homes. Check the website for schedules and stops.

XTREME ACTION PARK

5300 N. Powerline Rd., Fort Lauderdale: 954-491-6265
www.xtremeactionpark.com
ADMISSION: varies
Just as the name says, this is the fastest indoor go karting around. This is an excellent facility with a friendly staff. Lots of fun.

YOUNG AT ART CHILDREN'S MUSEUM

751 SW 125th Ave., Davie: 954-424-0085
Admission fee varies
Any day you drop in to the museum will be fun as they have different classes, workshops and exhibit. Very educational with areas like Earthworks that teaches children about recycling and repurposing and Global Village that teaches about different cultures through art, music and play.

Chapter 6
SHOPPING & SERVICES

BARNES & NOBLE BOOKSTORE
2051 N. Federal Hwy., Fort Lauderdale: 954-561-3732
http://www.barnesandnoble.com
Two-story mega bookstore has a Starbucks Coffee with
tasty desserts.

BASS PRO SHOPS OUTDOOR WORLD
200 Gulf Stream Way, Dania Beach: 954-929-7710
http://www.basspro.com

This store has an indoor water feature that showcases fish species that are indigenous to the area. The fish in their tanks are game fish of great size. In some of these aquariums, professional anglers and store staff hold demonstrations showing the use of artificial bait. They catch the fish in these tanks to show how well the bait works. Bass Pro Shops is also known for its Outdoor Skills Workshops, teaching skills as varied as fly fishing, Dutch oven cooking, archery hunting with an archery range in the store, and GPS navigation. They hold many "skill workshops" with the top names in the outdoor world. One of the really unique places to visit in the Fort Lauderdale not duplicated elsewhere in the country.

WESTFIELD BROWARD MALL
8000 W. Broward Blvd., Plantation: 954-473-8100
www.westfield.com/broward
Very nice mall, with Macy's, Dillards, Sears. Even Sears Auto. Nail and hair salon. Food court has the usual "variety," but nothing you've not seen before. Cuban to pizza to Chinese. Has lots of sales.

CORAL RIDGE MALL
3200 N. Federal Hwy., Fort Lauderdale: 954-537-2700
http://www.mycoralridgemall.com
You'll find values galore along with a wide range of services, food and entertainment at the Coral Ridge Mall. Centrally located in Greater Fort Lauderdale with easy access to the beaches. The mall is home to more than 40 stores and terrific prices and selections. Shop Target, Marshalls, HomeGoods, Old Navy, TJ Maxx, GNC, Payless ShoeSource, Bath & Body Works, Game Stop, Nine West, Footlocker, Easy Spirit and Motherhood Maternity just to name a few, plus Einstein Bros. Bagels, Jamba Juice, Galaxy Pizza, Publix and much more. Or stop by at AMC Movie Theatres for a cool escape.

DESIGN CENTER OF THE AMERICAS (DCOTA)
1855 Griffin Rd., Dania Beach: 954-920-7997
http://www.dcota.com
A 775,000-square-foot interior-design center with furniture
showrooms (featuring everything from ultramod to
classic), designer studios, and, from time to time, fabulous
sample sales.

DOLLAR TREE
1391 SE 17th St., Fort Lauderdale: 954-523-8397
http://www.dollartree.com
A true dollar store. Everything's $1. (Well, almost.) Among
the many, many items here you will find stuff like name
brand toothpaste. But if you're not shopping for toothpaste,
you will definitely find something you need. Clean and
well-organized store.

FORT LAUDERDALE SWAP SHOP
3291 W. Sunrise Blvd., Fort Lauderdale: 954-791-7927
www.floridaswapshop.com
This is a Flea Market but done on a much grander scale
than any other flea market. About the only thing you can't
find here are high prices. They have just about everything
from fresh produce, trashy junk, a few high-end items,

restaurants, car displays, drive-in movies, and sometimes, a circus show. (In fact, this place is a circus.)

GALLERIA MALL

2414 East Sunrise Blvd., Fort Lauderdale: 954-564-1036
http://www.galleriamall-fl.com
This is the place for Lauderdale's high-end shoppers. You make do here until you can visit Bal Harbour in Miami or Palm Beach. In fact, one of the reasons Fort Lauderdale doesn't have a huge number of high-end boutiques and specialty stores is because it lies so conveniently between Miami and Palm Beach, both of which have plenty of the best shopping in the world. The Galleria is anchored by three major department stores: Neiman Marcus, Macy's and Dillard's. Other famous retailers and specialty shops include Apple, Coach, Mayor's, Willams-Sonoma, Cole Haan, J.Crew and Pottery Barn. The Galleria is also a premier Fort Lauderdale dining destination, with restaurants like **Capital Grille, P.F. Chang's, Seasons 52, Blue Martini and Trulucks.**

GALLERY AT BEACH PLACE

17 S. Fort Lauderdale Beach, Fort Lauderdale: 954-760-9570

http://www.galleryatbeachplace.com

The area's only beachfront mall is located in Fort Lauderdale on Florida A1A just north of Las Olas Boulevard. This 100,000-square-foot giant has the usual chains, such as Sunglass Hut, as well as chain bars and restaurants such as Hooter's. While views of the ocean are fantastic, the shopping isn't so great, with only about 12 stores, one of them being a CVS Pharmacy that is open 24 hrs.

IKEA

151 NW 136th Ave., Sunrise: 888-888-4532

http://www.ikea.com/us/en/store/sunrise

The 20-acre Ikea store features exclusively designed items, three model homes, 50 room settings, a supervised children's play area, as well as a restaurant serving Swedish specialties as well as American dishes.

JEZEBEL
1980 E. Sunrise Blvd., Fort Lauderdale: 954-761-7881
They have a Facebook page
This funky, adorable shop is chock full of hip gifts, oodles of cards, designer and vintage clothing and accessories, and so much more. At Jezebel you'll find everything from stylish candles and home decor to funky jewelry and t-shirts, and everything in between.

LAS OLAS BOULEVARD
A block east of Federal Hwy. (US 1, off SE 8th St.), Fort Lauderdale
http://www.lasolasboulevard.com
Las Olas isn't just a street. The Boulevard begins with the Museum of Art at No. 1, and goes right down to the **Elbo Room** on A1A. In between the two are the businesses and organizations that you'd find in any other community in America; restaurants of all types, salons, banks, realtors, gas stations, a barbershop, a post office, a pharmacy, a deli, sidewalk cafes, jewelry stores, a cigar bar, antiques stores, art stores, fashion boutiques, a bakery, churches, shoe stores, a diner, a hotel, liquor stores, and even their own historic house.

LAS OLAS OUTDOOR GOURMET MARKET
1201 SE Las Olas Blvd., Fort Lauderdale
www.themarketcompany.org
This is a year-round open-air market featuring gourmet-style fruits and vegetables, organics, culinary herbs, tropical plants and orchids, fresh baked breads and pastries, local honey, handmade soaps, gourmet pastas, sauces and dressings, stone crabs in season, dog treats, and God knows what else.

LAS OLAS RIVERFRONT
Andrews Ave. at SE 2nd St., Fort Lauderdale: 954-522-6556
This was once a very nice place to spend an afternoon and evening. It is now a mere shadow of its former self and maybe not even that good. Only one decent restaurant still exists, the **Briney Pub.** You can pick up the water taxi there which is nice and there is a very good river cruise boat, but that's about it. In the evening, it is a hangout for rude kids and panhandlers.

OUT OF THE CLOSET
1785 E. Sunrise Blvd., Fort Lauderdale: 954-462-9442
www.outofthecloset.org
This place has really nice, gently used stuff. Clothes, furniture and knick-knacks for great prices. Every day there is a different sale, depending on the tag color. Sometimes you can get stuff for $1. All their proceeds go to AIDS/HIV research and you can also get a free HIV test after you shop.

RADIO-ACTIVE RECORDS

845 N. Federal Hwy., Fort Lauderdale: 954-762-9488
http://radio-active-records.tumblr.com
It's a bit bigger than your average record store. Pretty evenly split between new and used stuff. Carrying both CDs and Vinyl, with a pretty nice selection of niche stuff; such as local bands, garage, and psychedelic. Two turntables in the corner allow you to sample everything you're interested in buying.

SAWGRASS MILLS MALL

12801 W. Sunrise Blvd., Sunrise: 954-846-2300
http://www.simon.com/mall/?id=1262
Passionate shoppers can be assured they'll find absolutely everything here: from electronics, fashion, shoes, surf wear and boards (one of the largest **Ron Jon's Surf Shops** is located here) to art prints, there's virtually nothing you couldn't find at Sawgrass Mills. Besides shopping, there are plenty of entertainment options such as a multiplex movie theater with 23 cinemas and countless restaurants ranging from Burger King to **Wolfgang Puck**.

VICTORIA'S ATTIC

1926 E Sunrise Blvd., Ft Lauderdale, 954-463-6774
Victorian to mid-century furniture—most on consignment—this is a prime spot in the area to source that new-but-old chest of drawers you need for your bedroom. Packed to capacity, when you find something you like, it's like finding hidden treasure.

YELLOW GREEN FARMERS MARKET
1940 North 30th Rd., Hollywood: 954-513-3990
www.ygfarmersmarket.com
All under one outdoor roof, Yellow Green is a true
farmer's market providing a bounty of seasonal, fresh
foods along with artisanal goods created by local artists
and craftsmen. Come support and chat with local farmers
and gain a deeper understanding of the many healthful and
environmental benefits of seasonal eating.

INDEX

Symbols

15TH STREET FISHERIES, 22
3030 OCEAN, 23

A

ACQUARIO, 24
AGAVE TACO BAR, 51
AIRPORT AREA, 18
ALCAZAR RESORT, 19
American, 33, 62
American (New)/, 45, 49
American (traditional), 61
ANTHONY'S RUNWAY 84, 24
ASIA BAY, 30
ATLANTIC HOTEL, 8
AT'S-A-PIZZA, 45

B

BAHIA MAR BEACH RE-SORT, 9
Barbecue, 45
Bar Grub, 62
BARNES & NOBLE BOOK-STORE, 86
BASS PRO SHOPS OUT-DOOR WORLD, 86
BEACH AREA, 8
BETTY'S SOUL FOOD RES-TAURANT, 52
BILLIE SWAMP SAFARI, 76
BILLY'S STONE CRAB, 31
BISTRO MEZZALUNA, 24
Bliss Spa, 15
BLONDIE'S SPORTS BAR, 69
BLUE MOON FISH CO., 32
BOATYARD, 33
BOKAMPER'S SPORTS BAR & GRILL, 64
BOMBAY CAFE, 53
BONNET HOUSE, 76
Briney Pub, 92
BROWARD MALL, 85
B'STRO ON THE BEACH, 31
BURLOCK COAST SEAFARE & SPIRITS, 33
BUTTERFLY WORLD, 77

C

CAFÉ MARTORANO, 25
CAFE SEVILLE, 34
CAFE VICO INC, 25
CAMBRIA SUITES, 19
CANYON RESTAURANT, 34
CAP'S PLACE, 35
CARLOS & PEPE'S 17TH ST CANTINA, 35
CASABLANCA CAFE, 36
CASA D'ANGELO, 25
CASA D'ANGELO RIS-TORANTE, 36
CASA FRIDA, 53
CHIMA BRAZILIAN STEAKHOUSE, 26
CHRISTINA WAN'S MAN-DARIN HOUSE, 37
CORAL REEF GUEST-HOUSE, 19
CORAL RIDGE MALL, 87
COURTYARD BY MARRI-OTT FORT LAUDER-

DALE OCEANFRONT HOTEL, **9**
CROWNE PLAZA FORT LAUDERDALE AIRPORT / CRUISE PORT, **21**
CRUISE SHIP DEPARTURE STAYS, **20**
CULTURE ROOM, **68**

D

DESIGN CENTER OF THE AMERICAS, **88**
DICEY RILEY'S, **68**
Diner, **33**, **41**, **50**, **59**, **61**, **62**
DOLLAR TREE, **88**
DOWNTOWN AREA, **17**
DOWNTOWNER, **37**

E

EBAR, **70**
EDUARDO DE SAN ANGEL, **38**
EGG N YOU DINER, **54**
ELBO ROOM, **70**
EL TAMARINDO CAFÉ, **38**
EXIT 66, **70**

F

FLANIGAN'S, **64**
FLORIDIAN RESTAURANT, **54**
FORT LAUDERDALE AIRPORT/CRUISE PORT INN, **21**
FORT LAUDERDALE ANTIQUE CAR MUSEUM, **77**
FORT LAUDERDALE SUN

TROLLEY, **77**
FORT LAUDERDALE SWAP SHOP, **88**
FRESH FIRST, **54**

G

GALLERIA MALL, **89**
GALLERY AT BEACH PLACE, **90**
GALT VILLAS, **9**
Gastropub, **58**
GAY LODGINGS, **18**
GILBERT'S 17TH STREET GRILL, **39**
Gluten-free, **54**
GONDOLAS WEST, **78**
GRANADA INN, **9**
GREATER FORT LAUDERDALE CONVENTION & VISITORS BUREAU, **7**
GREEK ISLANDS TAVERNA, **39**
GULFSTREAM PARK RACING & CASINO, **78**

H

HAMPTON INN FT. LAUDERDALE DOWNTOWN, **17**
Heavenly Spa by Westin, **16**
HILLSBORO INLET LIGHTHOUSE, **78**
HOLIDAY INN EXPRESS AIR AND SEA PORT, **20**
HOLIDAY INN FORT LAUDERDALE AIRPORT, **18**
HUGH TAYLOR BIRCH

STATE PARK, **79**
HYATT REGENCY PIER
    66, **10**

I

IKEA, **90**
INDIGO, **40**
INTERNATIONAL SWIM-
    MING HALL OF
    FAME, **80**
Italian, **42, 57**

J

JACK'S OLD FASHION
    HAMBURGER
    HOUSE, **55**
JEZEBEL, **91**
Jimmy Evert Tennis Center,
    16
J. MARK'S RESTAURANT &
    BAR, **40**
JUNGLE QUEEN RIVER-
    BOAT, **80**
JWB PRIME STEAK, **27**

K

KELLY'S LANDING, **40**
KURO, **41**

L

LA BAMBA, **41**
LADY HELEN FISHING
    CHARTERS, **81**
LAGO MAR RESORT, **11, 24**
LANDLUBBERS RAW BAR
    & GRILL, **64**
LAS OLAS BOULEVARD,
    81, 91

LAS OLAS OUTDOOR
    GOURMET MARKET,
    91
LAS OLAS RIVERFRONT,
    81, 92
LA SPADA'S ORIGINAL
    HOAGIES, **56**
LAS VEGAS CUBAN CUI-
    SINE, **41**
LEMONGRASS ASIAN BIS-
    TRO, **42**
LE PATIO, **56**
LESTER'S DINER, **56**
LOBSTER BAR SEA GRILLE,
    27
LOUIE BOSSI'S RISTORAN-
    TE BAR PIZZERIA,
    42

M

MAI-KAI POLYNESIAN
    DINNER SHOW, **43,
    82**
MARIO'S CATALINA RES-
    TAURANT, **43**
MARKET 17, **44**
MARRIOTT'S BEACH-
    PLACE TOWERS, **11**
MCGINNIS WATERSKI,, **82**
MCSORLEY'S BEACH PUB,
    65
Mexican, **51, 53, 60**
MILLER'S ALE HOUSE, **65**
MOJO, **44**
MUSEUM OF DISCOVERY
    & SCIENCE, **83**

N

NEW TIMES, 7

O

OLD DILLARD CULTURAL ARTS MUSEUM, 83
OLD FORT LAUDERDALE VILLAGE & MUSEUM, 84
O LOUNGE, 70
ORIGINAL FAT CAT⊠S, 71
OUT OF THE CLOSET, 92

P

PARROT, THE, 71
Pier 66, 10
PILLARS, 12, 48
PIRATE REPUBLIC SEAFOOD & GRILL, 57
Pizza, 57
PIZZA CITY, 45
PIZZACRAFT ARTISAN PIZZERIA, 57
POOR HOUSE, 71
POSH LOUNGE, 72
PRESS GOURMET SANDWICHES, 58

Q

QUARTERDECK, 67

R

RADIO ACTIVE RECORDS, 93
RAINBOW PALACE, 45
RED CARPET INN, 20
RED COW, 45
REVOLUTION LIVE, 72

RHYTHM & VINE, 72
RITZ CARLTON FORT LAUDERDALE RESORT, 13
Riverside Hotel, 40
RIVERSIDE HOTEL, 17
RIVERSIDE MARKET SOUTH, 58
Riverwalk, 9
ROCK BAR, 72
Ron Jon's Surf Shops, 93
ROUND UP COUNTRY WESTERN BAR, 73
RUSTIC INN CRABHOUSE, 46

S

SAGE FRENCH CAFÉ AND OYSTER BAR, 47
Sandwiches, 58, 62
SAWGRASS MILLS MALL, 93
Sea Chateau Motel, 19
Seafood, 27, 29, 31, 32, 33, 35, 57, 60
SEA LORD HOTEL & SUITES, 14
SEASONS 52, 47
Secret Garden, 13
SECRET GARDEN, 48
SEMINOLE HARD ROCK HOTEL & CASINO, 73
SEVILLE HOTEL, 14
SHO NIGHTCLUB, 73
SHOOTERS, 74
SLACKERS BAR & GRILL, 66
Small Plates, 49
SMOKE BBQ, 59

Smoothies, **54**
SOUTHPORT RAW BAR,
    60
Spa Atlantic, **9**
Spanish, **53**
Steak 954, **15**
STEAK 954, **28**
Steakhouse, **27, 29**
STOUT BAR & GRILL, **66**
STRANAHAN HOUSE, **84**
SUBLIME, **49**
SUN-SENTINEL, **7**
SUSHI ROCK CAFE, **29**
SWEET NECTAR CHAR-
    COAL GRILL AND
    SPIRITS, **49**

T

Tapas, **49**
TARKS OF DANIA BEACH,
    62
TARPON BEND, **63**
TIMPANO, **50**
TOP HAT DELICATESSEN,
    61
TREASURE TROVE, **61**
TROPIROCK RESORT, **14**

V

VALENTINO'S CUCINA
    ITALIANA, **29**
Via Luna, **14**
VIBE LAS OLAS, **74**
VICTORIA'S ATTIC, **93**

W

WARSAW COFFEE COM-
    PANY, **62**
WATER TAXI, **84**

WESTFIELD BROWARD
    MALL, **87**
WESTIN BEACH RESORT
    FORT LAUDER-
    DALE, **16**
Westin Kids Club, **16**
WestinWORKOUT Gym, **16**
W HOTEL FORT LAUDER-
    DALE, **15**
WILD SEA OYSTER BAR &
    GRILLE, **29, 50**
Wolfgang Puck, **93**
WRECK BAR, **74**

X

XTREME INDOOR KART-
    ING, **85**

Y

Yellow Cab, **5**
YELLOW GREEN FARMERS
    MARKET, **94**
YOUNG AT ART CHIL-
    DREN'S MUSEUM,
    85

Other Books by the Same Author

Andrew Delaplaine has written in widely varied fields: screenplays, novels (adult and juvenile), travel writing, journalism. His books are available in quality bookstores as well as all online retailers.

JACK HOUSTON / ST. CLAIR POLITICAL THRILLERS

THE KEYSTONE FILE – PART 1
THE KEYSTONE FILE – PART 2
THE KEYSTONE FILE – PART 3
THE KEYSTONE FILE – PART 4
THE KEYSTONE FILE – PART 5
THE KEYSTONE FILE – PART 6
THE KEYSTONE FILE – PART 7 *(FINAL)*

On Election night, as China and Russia mass soldiers on their common border in preparation for war, there's a tie in the Electoral College that forces the decision for President into the House of Representatives as mandated by the Constitution. The incumbent Republican President, working through his Aide for Congressional Liaison, uses the Keystone File, which contains dirt on every member of Congress, to blackmail members into supporting the Republican candidate. The action runs from Election Night in November to Inauguration Day on January 20. Jack Houston St. Clair runs a small detective agency in Miami. His father is Florida Governor Sam Houston St. Clair, the Republican candidate. While he tries to help his dad win the election, Jack also gets hired to follow up on some suspicious wire transfers involving drug smugglers, leading him to a sunken narco-sub off Key West that has $65 million in cash in its hull.

THE RUNNING MATE

Sam Houston St. Clair has been President for four long years and right now he's bogged down in a nasty fight to be re-elected. A Secret Service agent protecting the opposing candidate discovers that the candidate is sleeping with someone he shouldn't be, and tells his lifelong friend, the President's son Jack, this vital information so Jack can pass it on to help his father win the election. The candidate's wife has also found out about the clandestine affair and plots to kill the lover if her husband wins the election. Jack goes to Washington, and becomes involved in an international whirlpool of intrigue.

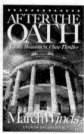

AFTER THE OATH: DAY ONE
AFTER THE OATH: MARCH WINDS
WEDDING AT THE WHITE HOUSE

Only three months have passed since Sam Houston St. Clair was sworn in as the new President, but a lot has happened. Returning from Vienna where he met with Russian and Chinese diplomats, Sam is making his way back to Flagler Hall in Miami, his first trip home since being inaugurated. Son Jack is in the midst of turmoil of his own back in Miami, dealing with various dramas, not the least of which is his increasing alienation from Babylon Fuentes and his growing attraction to the seductive Lupe Rodriguez. Fernando Pozo addresses new problems as he struggles to expand Cuba's secret operations in the U.S., made even more difficult as U.S.-Cuban relations thaw. As his father returns home, Jack knows Sam will find as much trouble at home as he did in Vienna.

THE ADVENTURES OF SHERLOCK HOLMES IV

In this series, the original Sherlock Holmes's great-great-great grandson solves crimes and mysteries in the present day, working out of the boutique hotel he owns on South Beach.

   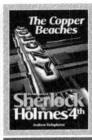

  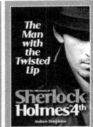 

THE BOSCOMBE VALLEY MYSTERY

Sherlock Holmes and Watson are called to a remote area of Florida overlooking Lake Okeechobee to investigate a murder where all the evidence points to the victim's son as the killer. Holmes, however, is not so sure.

THE DEVIL'S FOOT

Holmes's doctor orders him to take a short holiday in Key West, and while there, Holmes is called on to look into a case in which three people involved in a Santería ritual died with no explanation.

THE CLEVER ONE

A former nun who, while still very devout, has renounced her vows so that she could "find a life, and possibly love, in the real world." She comes to Holmes in hopes that he can find out what happened to the man who promised to marry her, but mysteriously disappeared moments before their wedding.

THE COPPER BEECHES

A nanny reaches out to Sherlock Holmes seeking his advice on whether she should take a new position when her prospective employer has demanded that she cut her hair as part of the job.

THE RED-HAIRED MAN

A man with a shock of red hair calls on Sherlock Holmes to solve the mystery of the Red-haired League.

THE SIX NAPOLEONS

Inspector Lestrade calls on Holmes to help him figure out why a madman would go around Miami breaking into homes and businesses to destroy cheap busts of the French Emperor. It all seems very insignificant to Holmes—until, of course, a murder occurs.

THE MAN WITH THE TWISTED LIP

In what seems to be the case of a missing person, Sherlock Holmes navigates his way through a maze of perplexing clues that leads him through a sinister world to a surprising conclusion.

THE BORNHOLM DIAMOND

A mysterious Swedish nobleman requests a meeting to discuss a matter of such serious importance that it may threaten the line of succession in one of the oldest royal houses in Europe.

SEVERAL TITLES IN THE DELAPLAINE SERIES OF PRE-SCHOOL READERS FOR CHILDREN

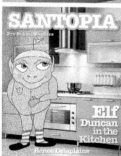

THE DELAPLAINE LONG WEEKEND TRAVEL GUIDE SERIES

Delaplaine Travel Guides represent the author's take on some of the many cities he's visited and many of which he has called home (for months or even years) during a lifetime of travel. The books are available as either ebooks or as printed books. Owing to the ease with which material can be uploaded, both the printed and ebook editions are updated 3 times a year.

Atlanta

Austin

Boston

Cancún (Mexico)

Cannes

Cape Cod

Charleston

Chicago

Clearwater – St. Petersburg

Fort Lauderdale

Fort Myers & Sanibel

Gettysburg

Hamptons, The

Hilton Head

Key West &
the Florida Keys

Las Vegas

Lima (Peru)

Louisville

Marseille

Martha's Vineyard

Memphis

Mérida (Mexico)

Mexico City

Miami & South Beach

Milwaukee

Myrtle Beach

Nantucket

Napa Valley

Naples & Marco Island

Nashville

New Orleans

Newport (R.I.)

Philadelphia

Portland (Ore.)

Provincetown

San Juan

Sarasota

Savannah

Seattle

Tampa Bay

THE FOOD ENTHUSIAST'S
COMPLETE RESTAURANT GUIDES

Atlanta

Austin

Barcelona

Boston

Buenos Aires

Cape Cod

Charleston

Chicago

Florence

Hampton, The

Houston

Key West &
the Florida Keys

Las Vegas

Lima (Peru)

London

Los Angeles

Louisville

Memphis

Mérida (Mexico)

Mexico City

Miami & South
Beach

Montreal

Napa Valley

Nashville

New Orleans

New York /
Manhattan

Paris

Philadelphia

Portland (Ore.)

Rome

San Diego

San Francisco

San Juan

Savannah

Seattle

Sonoma County

Tampa Bay

Toronto

Vancouver

Washington, D.C.

NOTES

CPSIA information can be obtained
at www.ICGtesting.com
Printed in the USA
BVHW080303111218
535235BV00015B/612/P

9 781640 226296